Harrogate Grammar School

A centennial history

Malcolm G. Neesam

Manor Place Press
Copyright Malcolm Neesam, 2003
Printed by Kolorco, Bradford

0 9510969 5 8

Throughout recorded human history, the ebb and flow of the love of achievement – and the resentment against its success – have been major forces behind the rise and fall of civilisations. While a civilisation is in ascendance (which is to say, when the morality of achievement has the upper hand), people tend to derive their cultural and social ideals from the class above them...But if and when resentment morality gains the upper hand, civilisation enters a slow decline... values from below begin to spread upward...
Robert Sheaffer,
Resentment against achievement

Contents

Introduction

Acknowledgements

Chapter one: Harrogate Grammar School's genesis,
                  1903 - 1914, pp. 7-19

Chapter two: The Great War, pp. 20-24

Chapter three: The Jazz age, 1919 - 1933, pp. 25-34

Chapter four: The impact of H.R.C. Carr, 1933 - 1939, pp. 35-44

Chapter five: The great days of "Tommy" Lusher, pp. 45-52

Chapter six: Post-war years, pp. 101-111

Chapter seven: 1950's – Mr. Carr's final decade, pp. 112-120

Chapter eight: The triumph of E.G. Hill, 1960 – 1980, pp. 121-137

Chapter nine: Enter Mary Dance, 1981 - 1991, pp. 138-144

Chapter ten: The century's passing - K. McAleese to
                  P. Limbert, 1992 – 2003, pp. 145-157

Author's postscript: pp. 158

Plates, pp. 53-100

Introduction

"Harrogate Grammar School – a centennial history" was the result of a January 2003 commission to the author to write the biography of a living institution that from its birth in 1903 has been at the heart of the Harrogate and district community. The school's wish to have the book available for the Centennial Ball at the Hotel Majestic on 20th September 2003 meant that the time available to the author for the book's research, writing, printing, binding and publication, was of necessity restricted. Consequently, the book's contents are based on information uncovered by the author between February and July 2003, including many contributions from pupils, staff and governors, both past and present.

This centennial history does not provide lists of all pupils, teachers or events connected to the school, so readers searching for the name of the head boy or girl for 1935, the winner of the high-jump competition in 1982, the painter of the stage sets for a school play production of 1909, or biographies of all favourite teachers, will be disappointed. Rather, the author has used a broad brush to depict the history of the school, set against a background of national developments in educational legislation, and the growth of the Harrogate community for which the Grammar School has been so central. And this last point needs to be appreciated. Harrogate has many excellent schools, some of which could have been established in any part of the country, where their intake of pupils would have been little different from that at Harrogate. These other establishments are simply schools located in Harrogate. Harrogate Grammar School, by its very nature, is unique, in that it was established as the town's principal state secondary school for higher education. Like Harrogate town and district, the Grammar School is a phenomenally successful institution, whose history has been a pleasure to uncover. Although the text has had to concentrate on the role of successive head teachers, the author has been made aware repeatedly of the splendid role of generations of skilled and motivated teachers, who, with the support of the often far-sighted board of governors, have enabled pupils to enter the adult world with the incomparable advantage of a sound education.

The author did not attend Harrogate Grammar School, and therefore had the advantage of writing its history in an unbiased and impartial frame of mind, unencumbered by childhood memories. Inevitably, some readers may find that later chapters of the book lack the charm of earlier ones, but this is because freedom of expression which so often produced colourful eccentricity, was reduced as society became more conformist and regulated. Equally, the fact that some of the players in the Grammar School's story are long dead, whereas others are very much alive, has quite properly had a restraining effect on the author's decision as to textual inclusion or exclusion.

The gathering and interpreting of material for this book within the constraints of an eight months time-frame, has meant that the author has not been able to contact all promising candidates, nor to integrate all material offered. Hence the author's adoption of the "broad-brush" approach to the writing of the Grammar School's history. The acknowledgements list recognizes the generosity of many individuals, and if the author has failed to include any names, the omission is purely accidental.

The quotation set next to the title page has been a rubric for the writing of this history. The majority of those involved with the running of the school for its first seventy years in existence would probably have applauded Robert Sheaffer's words. For the last thirty years, however, the majority would probably have been offended by them. The tension produced by this difference is central to understanding the Grammar School's history.

Opinions expressed in this book are those of the author, unless credited to other sources, and may not coincide with those of any other person.

Before the author began to work on this book, he knew from his own experience that individual teachers can be inspirational, but when he ended it, he had come to understand that establishments too can be inspirational.

Malcolm G. Neesam,
Manor Place, 2003.

Acknowledgements

I am grateful to many people for the information and material provided for the writing of this book, and am aware of useful contributions from anonymous donors, as well as from those who provided signed statements. To all contributors, I offer my profound gratitude, as it is thanks to their efforts that the writing of this history has been made possible. Alas, it has not been possible to name all the individuals who have aided me in the work of fulfilling the Grammar School's commission, but this must not prevent me from identifying those who have been especially cooperative: *Carol Arthur, Jean Barnstead, Mary Barker, Peter Barnwell, Alan Bassham, Donald S. Bell, Russell Betts, Audrey Bottomley, Roger Bottomley, and other members of the Bottomley family, Matthew Bourne, Colin Brittan, Philip Broadbank, George Capel, J.M. Clarke, Michael Clayton, Ruth Coombes, Shirley Cooper, Wendy Cross, Mary Dance, Russell Davidson, Margaret Eves, George R. Fowler, June Freeman, Barrie Heads, Ralph H. Hebbron, Barbara Hibbert, George Holmes, Eric H. Iveson, Monica Jenkins, Dr.Philip Limbert, Kenneth Lowe, Norman Lusher, Kevin McAleese, Margaret McGeorge, Adrian M.Mosley, Henrik Murden, J. Allan Patmore, D. Potts, Margery Raisbeck, Fred Roberts, Keith Sharman, K. Smith, Hugh B. Sykes, W.E. Tansley, Christine Toulson, Gordon Town, Geoff Wilkinson.* It would be churlish not to offer special thanks to five people who have had an important role in the final appearance of this book: Matthew Bourne of "Colour It In" for his expertise in preparing the illustrations and jacket; Wendy Cross of Harrogate Grammar School for her unfailing advice and encouragement; Russell Davidson, of Davidson Webber Ltd, solicitors, for his advice on textual matters; Jon Sewell and "Kolorco" for printing this book to such a high standard and within the limits of a tight timetable; and Dr. Philip Limbert, the Grammar School's current head teacher, who has been accommodating and encouraging over and beyond anything I might have expected. To all these individuals, and any others I have omitted inadvertently, I give my sincere thanks.

The illustrative material has been supplied either from the Grammar School's own archive, or from private sources, and it is unfortunate that many photographs did not possess captions or dates: in such cases, the author has been obliged to guess.

Chapter one

Harrogate Grammar School's genesis, 1903 - 1914

Harrogate, at the opening of the twentieth century, was reaping the benefits of many years of wise development of the community's incomparable natural resources. The town was riding on the crest of the wave of Victorian prudence, self-confidence and national pride, and was actively embracing the grand expansionism and investment that would in later eyes so typify the Edwardian age. One of Harrogate's most important resources was naturally its next generation, and the town participated in the national enthusiasm for building schools and colleges, training teachers, and applying legislation to meet the new century's aspirations.

The national census for 1901 showed that Harrogate's population had reached 26,583, a phenomenal growth since the estimated figure for 1801 of some 1,600 residents. The town's development, especially during the second half of the nineteenth century, was not unusual, thanks to the triple effects of an increasing population, improvements in public health, and mass transportation available through the superb railway system. Harrogate's growth differed from other communities, in that until the middle of the nineteenth century, the population consisted of a small number of the prosperous middle-classes (largely doctors and innkeepers) who provided amenities and services for the seasonal visitors to the Spa, who outnumbered the residents during the "Season". Both residents and visitors had access to a substantial servant class, many of whom were employed on a seasonal basis, migrating to and from their homes as the "Season" opened and closed. Accordingly, Harrogate children who might benefit from a Grammar School education were insufficient in number to merit the establishment within the town of a traditional Grammar School of the type already available in neighbouring Knaresborough. Private establishments such as Ashville gave fee-paying pupils access to the best education money could buy, and other able children, such as the future celebrated artist William Powell Frith, were sent to boarding schools away from Harrogate.

Around the year 1860, Great Britain probably reached her industrial peak, so far as concerned the genius of her people to develop and exploit national resources and technological innovation. After c.1880, a decline occurred, when the nation was overtaken by both Germany and the United States of America, a decline that was apparent to the late Victorian age's governments and educationalists. Significant steps to remedy this decline included the establishment in 1870 of rate-supported elementary schools, administered by school-boards, and the passing in 1880 of the Mundella education act that introduced compulsory schooling. In Harrogate, the authorities implemented the new Acts - which were concerned primarily with elementary education - with enthusiasm and efficiency. During this time, secondary education, when it was not in the hands of the private sector, was developed by the arts and technical colleges, which were to some extent a development of the old Mechanics' Institutes. It is instructive to compare the growth and role of Mechanics Institutes in towns similar to Harrogate. In areas amidst the working class populations of West Yorkshire and Lancashire, Mechanics' Institutes formed a bed-rock for past recipients of primary education. In Harrogate, with its low proportion of the classes for whom such institutes were a vital ingredient towards self-improvement, the Mechanics' Institute appeared to be little more than a vehicle for novelty and entertainment. The difference is instructive because it explains why Harrogate, until its population reached 20,000 towards the end of the nineteenth century, had no need for secondary education beyond that provided by the booming private sector. In one of its editions for May 1899, the Harrogate Advertiser carried advertisements for no fewer than nineteen private schools. Ten years earlier, the Technical Instruction Act had paved the way for improvements in secondary education nationally, and in 1891, Lord Salisbury's Act abolished fees in state schools. The way was then open for important developments in secondary education.

The year 1897 was in several respects a high-water mark for Harrogate. The Royal Baths were opened with great pomp and ceremony as Europe's most advanced centre for Hydrotherapy, and significant moves were taken towards the creation of a Kursaal, thanks to such luminaries as Samson Fox. Queen Victoria's Diamond Jubilee was celebrated with an enthusiasm that permeated every level of society. In March 1897, the Western Board School opened in Cold Bath Road, followed in October by Grove Road School, both schools having a combined capacity of 2,200, which when added to the town's voluntary schools, produced a figure of 3,300 pupils. Education was certainly in the air, both for the eminently practical reason of upgrading the local work-force, as well as the patriotic one of keeping abreast of Germany and the USA. Consequently, it was understandable that Harrogate's official celebrations to mark "the reign of the greatest sovereign of our nation's history", should have included the erection of a school for art and technology, a combination that the late Prince-Consort would surely have approved.

Some fifteen years before the 1897 Diamond Jubilee, the Harrogate Technical Instruction Committee had taken premises in Cambridge Crescent, opposite St. Peter's Church. It was funded partly by grants from the Department of Science and Art in South Kensington, and partly by the product of a local half-penny rate. Thomas Watson, ARCA, was in charge, who established classes for men and women that became so popular that calls were soon forthcoming for improved facilities, which peaked shortly before the 1897 jubilee.

In April 1897, a public meeting in the Council Chamber gave overwhelming support to the suggestion that part of the town's celebrations to mark the Queen's Jubilee, should include the erection of a School of Art and Technology. The following month the Council ratified the motion, and in October, the committee charged with administering the Diamond Jubilee celebrations handed to the Council a cheque for nearly £500 for the purpose of assisting the creation of a Harrogate School of Art and Technology. After slow progress, the foundation stone of the new building was laid on 19th December 1898 by the Honourable H.E. Butler of Nidd Hall, on a site at Haywra Crescent, surrounded by substantial mansions and terraces from the late Victorian age, and opposite the site of the new church for the Primitive Methodists. The school and the church were both the work of architect W.J. Morley, whose work was, in each case, selected in open competition by professional assessors, and it is unfortunate that such an important addition to the urban landscape was, at first, reduced in c.1969, when the church was demolished, and then destroyed, when the college was demolished in 1995. But back in the early twentieth century, the new buildings were regarded as ornaments to the town, and when the school on Heywra Crescent was ready, it was inevitably Thomas Watson, head of the old Department of Science and Art, who was appointed headmaster. Yet even before the first classes were held, the government was examining the whole matter of secondary education, the outcome of which would have dramatic implications for Harrogate's Art and Technical College.

In 1902, a new Education Act was passed, known as the Balfour-Morant Act, which had been devised by R.L. Morant, and taken up by Prime Minister Balfour as one of the beacons of his administration. The 1902 Act was an integral part of Balfour's vision for national efficiency, and ensured that County and County Borough Councils became the local authority for all state secondary and technical education. The same applied to elementary education, save that here, the councils of non-County Boroughs with populations of over 10,000, and urban districts of over 20,000, were to be the education authorities within their area. Henceforth, board schools and voluntary schools were brought under the control of the new Local Education Authorities, of which 140 were established. It was this recognition of local responsibility for the provision of public secondary education that stimulated the growth of higher education within the United Kingdom.

Harrogate Corporation responded quickly to the Balfour-Morant Act, and within days, the Town Clerk, Joseph Turner-Taylor recommended that a sub-committee be formed to look into the provisions of the new legislation, and the implications for Harrogate. At this point, the town was responsible for schools at Grove Road, Cold Bath Road, Starbeck, Bilton, Pannal and Beckwithshaw, the grant from government being on average slightly double the cost to the local rates. For example, Bilton board school received a government grant for 1902-3 of £370.9s.6d, the Council's grant being

£161.10s. The so-called "voluntary" schools that provided education along with the board schools, formed a second part of the machinery of education, and often had their origins in some charitable or sacred foundation. After 1902, all state schools passed into the control of the Local Education Authorities.

Despite the Council's initial response to the Balfour-Morant Act, further progress was slow, possibly because of the effects of other endeavours, such as absorbing the borough boundary additions of 1900, planning and building the Kursaal between 1898 and 1903, completing the gigantic reservoir and water distribution system, and ensuring that the eight senior and seven infants schools, run since 1897 by the municipality, were administered satisfactorily.

Harrogate's School Board was dissolved on 1st April 1902, after some eleven years excellent service, and one week later, the "Herald" reported one of the first recommendations of the new Education Committee: that the Council should take over Harrogate Technical College, clearly with an eye to implementing the Balfour-Morant Act. Shortly after this, a prospectus appeared in the newspapers that showed the Committee had been busy: *Resolution has been passed by Harrogate Council that a secondary school shall be commenced after the summer season. The school will be a secondary day school for boys and girls, under the inspection of the Board of Education and the West Riding County Council...the object of the school is to prepare youths for industrial, commercial and professional pursuits. It will supply a sound general modern education, from the sixth standard of an elementary school, to the work required for matriculation at the universities. Classes from 9.00am to 12.15, and 2.00 to 4.30pm, except Saturdays. A certain amount of homework must be done by each pupil."*

During the early years of the twentieth century, Harrogate was experiencing something of a growth of interest in religious nonconformity, in contrast to the years before c.1850, when the town was almost unique in northern England in being a bastion of Anglicanism. Conscious of their newly acquired clout, the non-conformists joined the "passive resistance movement", which was an ultimately unsuccessful effort to wriggle out of their social responsibility of paying taxes, on the grounds that some taxes funded education, and some education included religious doctrine unpalatable to non-conformist opinion. Religious instruction was provided at the new "Municipal Secondary School" from the start, but it never dominated the curriculum in the obsessive manner of some other establishments.

In August 1903, Harrogate Council heard that the government did not expect the clauses of the new act, insofar as secondary education was concerned, to be implemented until 1st April 1904, but on the 16th September, an advertisement appeared in the Harrogate Herald announcing: *"Harrogate technical School. Session 1903-4. Commencing 21st September. The Committee have pleasure in announcing that the staff of teachers has been considerably augmented and that additional facilities are now offered to all students ...(the) Secondary Day School [new department] will provide a thorough scientific and general education for both boys and girls from the work of the sixth standard in an elementary school to that required for matriculation in the universities...".* As publicity for the new school appears to have been minimal, the first intake was probably very small.

Harrogate Council spent much of the Autumn of 1903 in forming the new Education Committee, and it was only in December that Councillor Amos Chippindale was elected chairman. On 9th December the Herald carried an advertisement for the "Municipal Secondary Day School": *"A new class commences in January"*. The vagueness of this announcement does not reveal much about the school, although a later writer recorded that the first known figure for school attendance was forty-four pupils.

Children who applied for admission by scholarship were required to take an examination in arithmetic, English and oral testing, with a maximum of 250 marks awarded. The surviving registers reveal that the majority of candidates were successful, although occasional annotations show that candidates with marks below 90 were rejected, accompanied by explanations such as *"too backward"* or even *"too old"*. This last comment indicates that if an older child obtained higher marks, they would have been accepted!

In 1904 the Board of Education in London issued regulations for secondary schools, which attempted to ensure that new secondary schools would follow closely the conventions and curricula of the old public and grammar schools. In retrospect, this may be seen as counter-productive, as it introduced to state education the concept of meddling in local affairs. Indeed, a case may be made for 1904 being the start of a disastrous trend for ever-increasing meddling in local education by the state, after the introduction of the very necessary reforms of 1870, 1891, and 1902.

Harrogate's unique nature ensured that *any* regulations introduced in far away London would not always be to the educational benefit of local children, especially such concepts as copying the conventions and curricula of the old public and grammar schools. At best, the old order was superb at producing a small number of brilliant statesmen to run the country like a personal fiefdom, but the spread of democracy, technology, mass transportation, and a consumerism allied to personal expectation, ensured that the educational system of the old order was not suitable for mass-transference over the entire country. All too often, attempts to mimic the old schools produced crumby institutions that had wonderful uniforms, school songs, and customs, and which taught their pupils innumerable sayings from classical authors. Such pupils often left school without an inkling of modern chemistry, engineering, physics, hygiene, or the glories of architecture or music. Yet these same pupils were expected to withstand the challenge from their counterparts in Germany and the United States of America.

The significance of Harrogate's unique nature lay in the following: as the population had only reached the level to support a Grammar School after c.1880, and the town's other places of secondary education were principally for the children of non-residents, the curriculum of the new Grammar School of 1903-4 should have been determined both by the *general* educational needs, as well as the *specific* employment potential of those Harrogate children. Specific *local* employment potential was largely in the commercial or professional sectors (retailing, management, medicine, architecture and building). Therefore, the provision of an education based on a traditional public school would have been all but useless.

The pupils who would attend the new Grammar School could have come from any part of the town, such as old localities like Well Hill or Church Square, or new ones like the neighbouring Dragon estate, developed by the Chippindale brothers, or the Regent estate, as well as the more affluent surroundings of the Tewit Well or Duchy estates. In 1903-4, children walked to school, although some from outlying parts came by train from Pateley Bridge, Hampsthwaite or Pannal. Whether or not the children approached the school from across the town centre, the Dragon estate, from High Harrogate, or across Sheepshanks's fields, opposite East Parade, they would have been aware of a changing landscape, as more and more houses gobbled up fields that had once been used by the big hotels as farms and gardens.

The Harrogate Municipal Secondary School accepted ten scholarship pupils during the financial year ending in March 1904, and on 12th May, the Education Committee was advised that Mr. Watson had asked for the ten to be continued, and for another ten to be added. His request was accepted. The men who sat on the Education Committee were largely drawn from the same class of men who ran the town, men who were builders by trade, Methodist by conviction and Liberal by persuasion, although the Conservatives and Anglicans were almost as powerful. The town over which these groups held sway was a fine town of stone houses, shops and hotels. The visitors were the mainstay of the economy, and so long as they continued to spend the "Season" filling the hotels and boarding houses, patronising the town's many excusive shops, drinking the Mineral waters in the pump rooms or bathing in the Royal or Victoria Baths, so would the town continue to thrive. From the crest of Ripon Road to St. Mark's Church on Leeds Road, or from Granby Corner to the brow of Harlow Hill,

Harrogate exuded an air of genteel wealth. It had no slums, and only two poor streets, and the green expanse of the Stray, Harrogate's greatest asset, stretched proudly round the town centre. Parks, gardens, and open countryside were available to all in abundance, and the scented air that blew over the town from the Pinewoods, added to the atmosphere of healthfulness and progress.

The contemporary Harrogate press records little about the first year of the Municipal Secondary School, probably because other local affairs dominated the news, such as the opening of the Kursaal and the Grand Hotel, the debate over a tramway system, and the interminable disagreements over the best way of providing improved accommodation at the Royal Pump Room.

Within three years, accommodation at the Municipal Secondary School was proving inadequate. When it opened, the school had four class rooms on the ground floor, and shared a science laboratory, art room and kitchen with the Art school. Physical training was done in the basement that also housed the Art School's clay and plaster work area.

At this period, teacher training included the concept of "pupil-teachers", who were drawn from the town's educational establishments. They were young people who desired to become school teachers in elementary schools, receiving certificates of commendation that enabled them to gain free admission to the Harrogate Municipal Secondary School to the age of sixteen. Subject to good progress reports, they were then able to enter the government's exam for pupil-teachers and if successful, were apprenticed for two years. As an incentive to further progress, a bonus was given to every pupil teacher entering a training college.

Headmaster Watson probably had a staff of only half a dozen teachers when the new school opened in 1903-4, a figure that grew as the school developed, so that by about 1910, the complement of staff reached thirteen full time teachers. These were the days of rigid gender separation, so an annual intake of boys and girls required teachers for each gender, to say nothing of the specialist staff for science, physical training or art. By 1905, probably as the result of the November inspection, effort was made to alleviate the crowding by renting accommodation at a house in East Parade, which soon came to be known as "the work house", and used to accommodate the oldest pupils. The "work house" enabled three extra school-rooms to be acquired as well as space for other activities, and it was at the "work house" that the first school dinners were prepared and cooked. This being Yorkshire, the meals were proper dinners, and not effete southern snacks, with a mouthful of lettuce and empty air. They consisted – at least in the palmy days before the Great War – of meat and vegetables – followed by a rib-sticking pudding.

Playtime breaks were at first held outside the school grounds, so that noise from children at play did not disturb the lessons of those working in the school building. A.C.T White recalled that East Parade and Bower Road were popular places to play, as well as neighbouring Sheepshanks Fields, which in those days filled the whole east side of East Parade. The streets were quite safe, as the only traffic to use them other than slow moving horses and carts, were the lumbering omnibuses on solid tyres, and if anyone had been knocked down by one, it would have served them right. In Harrogate, horses still dominated transportation, and one teacher was said to bring his old chestnut mare into the school in hard weather !

The school had grounds within its walls, which seem to have been reserved for the youngest of the children, again segregated by gender. One pupil later recorded the fright everyone received when a huge elm tree, that stood on the dividing line, quite suddenly and unexpectedly, toppled slowly over during one playtime. Amazingly, no one was injured.

Schools in Harrogate that were supported out of public funds were also open to inspection by any member of the public, on the grounds that people were entitled to see how their money was being spent. It was theoretically possible for a school to be inspected by any rate-payer at any time, although in reality, such inspections were probably rare occurrences. Official inspections were another matter, and after the inspection of 1910, the report noted that Harrogate's Municipal Secondary School was *"a pearl of a school in a pigsty of a building"*, a criticism that undoubtedly resulted from crowding two separate schools into a building intended for only one. It was probably as a result of the 1910 inspection that steps were taken in 1911 to improve matters. The following summer, the school was enlarged with another storey, designed with modern plate-glass windows to admit the maximum amount of light. As well as extra class-rooms, a new handwork area was provided, together with a cloakroom, large gymnasium, and playground enclosed by a high stone wall. Change also occurred when Mr. Watson left his post, moving back into the old school of art, and staff member A.E. Thoseby, who had been on the staff since the school opened, became headmaster.

Around 1910, the school issued the first edition of its magazine. Unfortunately, none have survived, so a useful source of information has vanished, but the second edition that appeared in the summer term of 1912, bemoaned the fact that the first edition had not sold well. Writing in the editorial column, headmaster Thoseby reminded pupils that the magazine was a record of school events that everybody should support. He also noted that in the year passed since moving into the enlarged premises, the annual number of entrants had increased from 184 to 222, an increase of over 20%. Subjects taught over and above the original core subjects included gym and drill, needlework, cookery, singing (but not, let it be noted music, and this at a time when England was at the height of its musical creativity), morris dancing, and swimming. This last was perhaps because of the proximity of the Dragon Parade Swimming Baths, which had re-opened in 1903 under the control of Harrogate Corporation. Boys could also have boxing lessons, although they were somewhat limited, probably because of the lack of qualified teachers. For some years, the timetable included a subject called "laboratory practice", which was an amalgam of chemistry and physics, but this seems to have been restricted to younger years, as older children had the two subjects taught separately.

Possibly with an eye to future potential employees, Mr. Woods of the famous linen emporium in Prince's Street, presented the school with a glazed display case containing samples of linen in various stages of manufacture that was no doubt used to good effect in Mr. Hislop's geography lessons. One unusual event was the appearance at the school of a body of *"West African natives, in native dress"* who provided a concert, that reinforced the children's awareness of Britain's world-wide imperial possessions. This of course was the hi-tide of imperialism and patriotism, and in common with schools throughout the empire, classroom maps were divided into areas that were red and British, and areas that were not. Pride in the nation's accomplishments was a natural part of the teaching method, and anyone not conforming was despised as a poor thing, or even worse, as a pro-boer!

The school magazine was entitled " The Harrogatonian", and in the second edition, reference was made to the *"school dinners, made famous by Mrs. Fallon. We boast that we provide the best sixpenny dinner in town"*. The editor did not explain why Mrs. Fallon's dinners were famous, so we shall be charitable and suggest that it was their high quality.

In 1912 the school's governors ordered that an honours board be erected in the assembly hall, so that pupils' best achievements could be commemorated, and other pupils see something to which they could aspire. Some thirteen names were inscribed, including, for 1910 achievements, that of A.A. Thomson, who later immortalised the school in his wonderful novel *"The Exquisite Burden"*. Another name that had been inscribed for 1908 achievement was that of Donald S. Bell, who became one of two ex- pupils to receive the Victoria Cross in the Great War.

On 5th January 1912, a re-union meeting was held for former pupils, that seems to have been such a success, that it became a regular activity, although one that needed the enthusiasm of a few individuals, rather than the support of the school's administration, who were too busy to attend to such pleasant fringe activities.

No child living in Harrogate should ever grumble about lack of playing fields, as the Stray has provided an incomparable flat grassy open space since 1778. However, an area more immediately convenient to a school never comes amiss, and the Secondary Municipal School was no exception, so a field was rented at the end of Walker's passage nearest East Parade. A later writer described it as being *"ribbed like corduroy"* and kept in order by *"a twelve inch mower and scythe"* Part of the field still exists at the time of writing, now being a public open space. By the 1920's, the Grammar School was holding larger sporting events on Goodrick's fields, Otley Road, which were also used for circuses and galas, but it is not known when this practice began.

The school magazine issued in the summer of 1912 contained an account of a new debating and literary society formed by pupils from forms va and vi. The school seems to have encouraged the art of debating, as pupil A.A. Thomson later recorded in his novel, "The Exquisite Burden" : *"...they were all members of the school, debating society, and made earnest speeches on tariff reform, conscription and women's suffrage, Freeth's principle was to teach boys to express their thoughts clearly and without self-consciousness...."* As for literature, the pupils had access not only to the classics, but to such moderns as P.G. Wodehouse, Arnold Bennet, Arthur Conan Doyle, Bernard Shaw and H.G. Wells, as A.A.Thomson recalled.

A poem, published in the school magazine for 1912, commemorated the dreadful loss of the Titanic, which certainly shook the confidence of the time, without necessarily appearing as a portent. Harrogate was at the peak of its exclusiveness, the streets being thronged with kings and queens, prime ministers and grand duchesses, mostly in mufti, a fact that was probably lost of the pupils, who were more concerned with the problems of everyday life. One matter that seems to have caught the attention of the new debating society was the vexed issue of accommodation at the Royal Pump Room, opened in 1842, which by the end of the century could no longer accommodate all who wished to gain admittance. Some favoured building a new enlarged structure, while others argued against anything that might disturb the sanctity of the geological strata beneath the Sulphur Well. The issue was finally resolved in 1913, when the Lord Mayor of London opened a new light-weight building of glass and iron that had been added to the pump room, a visit that became a subject for essay writing at the Municipal Secondary School!

The issue of the Harrogatonian for February 1913 contained results for the previous season's examinations, including English composition, Latin, French, history, geography, arithmetic, algebra, geometry, chemistry, drawing, religious knowledge, physics (for boys) or domestic science (for girls), and for forms 11, 11b, and 111a only, general elementary science. At the same time, the school upgraded the significance of non-academic pursuits by erecting a sports board in the school gymnasium with the names of those who won their colours at football, cricket and hockey. Indeed, the magazine reported that the annual school sports day *"at the field in West End Avenue"* (Goodrick's field) had been unusually well attended that year.

During the spring term of 1914, the school's headmaster Mr. Thoseby, introduced a new prefectorate, whereby the student teachers were joined by four boys and eight girls to share the responsibilities of the office. These included the privilege of reading the lesson at prayers, and of supervising delinquents in the detention rooms. Other means of dealing with unacceptable behaviour included teachers overawing their pupils by means of speech tone or body language, such as was the hall-mark of the French teacher, Monsieur Jacot or the use of corporal punishment by the headmaster, using a standard cane issued by the West Riding County Council to all schools within their inspectorate. At this time, and for some years to come, corporal punishment was accepted by society as a cheap and sensible way of maintaining order in schools, the criminal courts and prisons, but thanks to such public figures as Mr. G.B. Shaw, voices could be heard calling for its abolition. Unlike the crumby private schools so harshly condemned by Winston Churchill in his book "My early life", or the insignificant ragged schools described by historian H.H. Walker in his recollections of a boyhood in Knaresborough, corporal punishment in Harrogate's Secondary Municipal Day School seems to have been infrequent and limited, although doubtless the victims would have disagreed.

The writing of this history has entailed the study of many written statements, conversations, and memoirs of former pupils, and of such recollections of the period before 1943, few fail to mention Monsieur Jacot, the French teacher, who was actually of Belgian nationality. Former pupil A.A. Thomson described Jacot under the disguise of Monsieur Merle, in his chapter "War with the French" *"Monsieur Merle could be charming. He could also be murderous. ...His appearance, form three considered, was most unfair, for he looked not unlike a Punch drawing of a French count. His tall hat and beautifully moulded frock-coat, his fiercely curled moustache and imperial (beard) were all of the essence of the fun-making froggies of fiction. Moreover, he rode to school every morning on a low framed bicycle, his frock-coat tail flapping out in the breeze behind him. All these things, it might have been argued, were expressly for the unholy delight of school boys...apart from his cyclonic wrath.. .he was also a superb teacher...".* A.A. Thomson went on to describe Monsieur in action *"...Form 3a worked for Monsieur Merle as it worked for no one else, from sheer terror...a suspected smile was the worst of crimes...the victim would be seized by the collar and shaken with such violence that it seemed that all his limbs would be jerked loose from their sockets. It was a terrifying form of punishment".*

Monsieur Jacot/Merle does not appear to have mellowed. A piece of school folklore recounts the time that the enraged Jacot threw a boy against the staircase with such force that a baluster broke, resulting in a parental visit to the school and Jacot's temporary suspension. Former pupil George Holmes, who attended the Grammar School from 1936 until 1942, recalls that he *"slept very badly during Wednesday night, as the class had two periods with Jacot the following day"*. Mr. Holmes was not alone with his feelings for Jacot. Fred Roberts, another ex-pupil, recalled that *"Monsieur Jacot tried to produce results from the class by frightening the living daylights out of us"*. Not all memories of Jacot are bad ones however, and for ex-pupil Mrs. M.R. Barker, he was *"a real character, who used to give favourite pupils a peppermint"*

It is self-indulgent folly to attempt to judge another age by the standards of today (any today), but regardless of when, or by whom such an assessment is made, the number and vehemence of adverse reports of Jacot's behaviour all point to the conclusion that the man was at the very least a bully, and probably worse. It is easy enough to be self-controlled when dealing with clever children who are keen to learn, but the good teacher should also be able to encourage and foster the less able, nervous or even stupid child, and such professionalism seems to have been beyond Jacot's ability. Teachers such as Mr. T.E. Kitching, the wood-work master, who joined the staff in January 1909, left a more agreeable impression, being a man of skill and patience. Some of Mr. Kitching's pupils eventually obtained work with local carpenters, such as those in Thompson's yard or the workshops of Topham brothers, and all the evidence points to the importance accorded to "blue collar" or technical work in the school's curriculum and timetable. The concentration on academic examination results that later became such a feature of Grammar School life, was unknown before the Great War. The practical side of girls' education was provided by Miss Wade, the needlework mistress, whose instruction gave her charges a means of future employment. Such work, although desperately hard, was at least permanent, as the skills of a seamstress were in regular local demand, as may be revealed by even a cursory examination of the Harrogate Advertiser.

In January 1914 the Board of Education sent five inspectors to the school, who produced a very appreciative report on progress, noting the contribution of the first Chairman of Governors, Mr. B.F. Brooke, who now had to resign for medical reasons. Councillor J.S. Rowntree was elected as a new chairman, an excellent choice, given his known commitment to secondary education, and his generosity as a public figure. This was at a time when the Harrogate population had increased by about a third since the beginning of the century, jumping from 26,583 in 1901 to 33,703 in 1911. In neighbouring Dragon Parade, for example, the number of homes increased from 27 to 76 in that first decade, a growth that over the whole urban area produced greater demand for such public amenities as transport, power, sewering, and recreational space. This last was one of Councillor Rowntree's special interests, and in 1914, when the Harlow Carr estate came on the market and the town council failed to acquire it for the public, it was Councillor Rowntree and two other councillors who purchased it for £8,500, and told Harrogate that they would keep it until the town could afford to buy it at the same price. Councillor Rowntree proved to an outstanding Chairman of the Board of Governors, and served as Mayor from 1911 to 1913.

During the summer of 1914, the school participated in a gymnastic competition with other schools supported by grants from the West Riding County Council, as well as playing in county football, cricket and hockey matches. Indeed, extra-curricula activities were on the increase, as shown by the formation of a dramatic society, and mass bicycle rides to Aldborough. By July 1914, the school had 274 pupils and 15 staff.

At a reunion for old students, held at the Grand Hotel in 1933, some of the names of these pupils were recalled: the formidable Wade brothers, "bully" Mitchell, Alec Scott, who invented body-line bowling, the star footballers George Philbey and Marcus Wilkinson, and *"those two noble knights, Donald S. Bell and Archie White, who went on to achieve national honour in the annals of both the school and the nation"*. Donald S. Bell had transferred to Harrogate's Municipal Secondary School from Knaresborough, where he had been a pupil at the King James' Grammar School.

Many of the pupils of Harrogate's Municipal Secondary School, in common with the rest of the town's youth, were probably preoccupied with matters aeronautical during the summer holidays. It had been three years since the round Britain air race of 1911 had welcomed the international team of aviators to Harrogate, who had landed on the south Stray in shockingly flimsy machines and to the plaudits of immense crowds. In June 1914 the hero of the hour was Mr. W. Rowland Ding, who not only arrived in a substantial Handley-Page biplane, but who gave townspeople the chance of a flight round the town at 6d a time. So popular were Mr. Ding's flights, that he was soon joined by aviator Harold Blackburn, whose dashing exploits made him every school boy's icon. However, a group of rate-payers objected to flights on Sundays, and also to the Stray being used as an aerodrome, so a petition was presented to the Council demanding that the flights should stop.

As the heat of July turned into the heat of August, the international situation began to deteriorate. Ex-pupil A.A. Thomson later recorded in his semi-autobiographical novel, the gathering of three chums at their favourite meeting place at the old stone bridge over Oak Beck. The three friends talked about the coming war *"just as they would have argued about football. Wars were declared by governments and fought by soldiers...never for one instant did the three lads on Oak Beck bridge see the war as something that might affect their own lives"*. A.A. Thomson's two friends were Donald S. Bell and Archie White, both of whom were to win the V.C., one posthumously.

Chapter two

The Great War

The issue of the Harrogatonian for December 1914 began with the words *"many changes have occurred since our last issue. Our country has been involved in a terrible war. Many of our old boys have responded nobly to their country's call...we are glad to see Monsieur Jacot again after his absence with the Swiss army. His place was temporarily filled by Madame Size...the pupils' Christmas concert has proceeded as before, but this time, a few Belgian friends were present ... patriotic songs sung included "It's a long way to Tipperary" and "Land of Hope and Glory". The whole school also sang the national anthems of our allies.*

Even before the outbreak of war on 4th August 1914, the school would have been gripped by a fever of speculation. Were Herr Otto Schwartz and his String Band really German spies?, was it true that there had been an attempt to poison the old Sulphur Well?, don't you think that the Kursaal's name should be changed to something English?, was the Grand Duchess George of Russia really who she said she was? Fuelled by this speculation, as well as by a heady brew of excitement and patriotism, it was absolutely inevitable that the crowds around the Raglan Street recruiting office, and the Strawberry Dale drill hall, were filled with young men fresh from their last year at school. Some may have been old enough to have signed up legally; others either forged their age, or were guided through the process by a knowing officer who admired their pluck. When they left Harrogate railway Station, the whole town turned out to wave them off.

The new Mayor of Harrogate, Alderman Sheffield, whose nickname of fishy-Joe came from his ownership of a Prince's Street Oyster bar, set about to organise relief funds to aid the war effort, and within a month of the war's beginning, pupils of the Municipal Secondary School were involved. They were encouraged to make things for the soldiers, and forty-five body belts and forty-eight pairs of socks were despatched from the school. Nor were the Belgians overlooked, and the wife of the chairman of the school's governors, Mrs Rowntree, arranged for twenty-eight scarves and two pairs of socks to be delivered, as well as two tins of chocolate from herself, presumably to Belgian refugees in England.

A number of refugees were received in Harrogate during the Autumn of 1914, including children. At the same time, the school co-operated with the Society of the Friends of Refugees, who had opened Roker House in Dragon Parade as a special home for fifteen refugees, and there is evidence to show that school children were given certain responsibilities for the occupants' welfare. It seems that some of the refugee children were admitted to the school, so much so that instructions were received from the Education Board that no more children be taken on to the school's registers, which then recorded 289 pupils. The school forms at this time were numbered 1, 2, 3a, 3b, 3c, 4a, 4b, 4c, 5a, 5b, and 6.

The school magazine continued to be issued through the war, and the Christmas edition noted, among several such reports, that old boy A.A. Thomson had enlisted in the Fifth West Yorkshire Regiment, and Donald S. Bell had enlisted in the West Yorkshire Light Infantry. As for old boy Jock Dawson, he was a prisoner of war at Ruhleben near Berlin, and would welcome letters or parcels addressed to barrack number seven.

The war's immediate impact on Harrogate emptied the great hotels of their staff, (many of whom were citizens of hostile powers) and caused some guests to depart before the end of the season. However, in general, the Spa carried on, unlike the outbreak of world war in 1939. During much of the First World War, the Council sponsored a detailed analysis and investigation of the town's famous mineral waters, ostensibly by Professor Smithells, but in reality by Arnold Woodmansey, a corporation official who in 1914 had been appointed as the town's resident expert chemist, a post re-graded after the war to that of Borough Analyst. These events occurred at a time when chemistry was regarded as a vital element of progressive national life. Before the war one of the greatest threats to the country's economic life was perceived to be the formidable German advances in chemistry and dye production. It may therefore be seen that the rise of chemistry's importance in the educational curriculum had established, as well as immediate causes, and Harrogate's Municipal Secondary School was no exception.

The school's chemistry laboratory had one or two adjoining smaller cubicals, that had been intended to provide a home for special equipment, experiments and course work, but senior master Edwin "Teddy" Morris had another use for them. The so-called "balance room" was where pupils were banished who had behaved in an "*ungentlemanly or ruffianly manner*", sitting in detention to reflect on the error of their ways.

Pupils do not seem to have experienced many immediate difficulties as a result of war-time conditions, other than the obvious ones of absent fathers or brothers. Extra-curricular activities continued, and indeed increased, as the school tried to develop its role in the community. On 3rd February 1916, the school arranged performances of scenes from "Alice in Wonderland", "L'Avocat Pathelin", and Sophocles "Antigone", the expenses of which were defrayed by the generous Councillor Rowntree, Chairman of the school's governors. During the summer of 1916, net-ball was introduced, the first march being against Birklands School. The interest in the girl guides' movement produced a special group based on the Municipal Secondary School, and known as the Third Harrogate Girl Guides' movement, who met for the first time on 3rd July, and had an enjoyable day at Plumpton Rocks. The group progressed, and were able to participate in the big inspection of over four hundred guides at Leeds by Miss Baden Powell, a gathering that included the new one from Harrogate.

During 1916, the school's pupils undertook a certain amount of work to support the war effort, including the girls' contribution of filling 300 sandbags that were sent to London. This was at a time when the dreadful reality of the war was looming over every street in the nation, as the casualty figures crept upward inexorably. In 1916, the school heard the fate of three old boys: first, from Captain Archie White, who visited the school while on sick-leave resulting from wounds received during the Dardanelles campaign. Other old boys were less fortunate, as the school learned on receiving news of Jack White, a Second Lieutenant in the Green Howards, who was mortally wounded at Suvla Bay, and of Edward Baker, a Corporal in the Fifth West Yorkshires, killed by a shell in August. By Easter 1916, the school magazine reported that Captain Archie White's friend, A.A. Thomson, now a Second Lieutenant in the Northumberland Fusiliers, was in Newcastle infirmary suffering from a knee injury. Another old boy, Norrie Beach, had gained the D.C.M. and Digby Chamberlain, a Lieutenant in the Royal Garrison Artillery, had been mentioned in despatches. The magazine also referred to three members of staff being on active service, Mr. Jones, Mr. Rogers and Mr. Kitching. In all, one hundred old boys were on war service, two had been killed in action, one died of wounds, and one died in training. There was no counselling; one had to simply accept.

In Harrogate, war service had become a well-established aspect of daily life. In March 1915, the Fifth West Yorkshire regiment, including many old boys such as Edward Baker, left the town for the front lines in France. The same month saw the Council discussing whether or not to change the name of the Kursaal, the decision being to leave it as it was. In June, the Young Men's Christian Association opened a Soldiers' Tent Club near Killinghall Camp, and March 1916 saw the first of Grand Duchess George of Russia's hospitals for wounded servicemen open in Dragon Parade, opposite the school's main premises. Then, in July 1916, the school learned of the death of Donald S. Bell, during the battle of the Somme. He won the VC on 5th July at Horseshoe Trench, just five days before being killed in action on 10th July 1916. Donald Bell never knew he had won the highest military honour the nation could bestow, but back in Harrogate, the news spread like wildfire.

1916 was also the year that Mrs.Lizzie Finzi moved to Harrogate, with her son, the future famous composer, Gerald Finzi, then aged fifteen. Young Finzi appears to have been taught privately, and it is one of this history's great "might-have-beens" to consider that he very nearly became the most famous pupil of the Municipal Secondary Day School. However, Finzi's delicate health ensured he received a private education.

The school magazines are missing for the period between Easter 1916 and Christmas 1917, but this latter edition shows something of the changing times, in that it seems to be the first edition with commercial advertising, and also the first to include a photograph, as distinct from a line drawing or wood cut, the subjects being the boys' football team, and the girls' hockey team. The retirement was announced of the Chairman of the school's board of Governors, Councillor Rowntree, who was leaving Harrogate, the new Chairman being Councillor Topham. This was at a time when the Board was active in its consideration of changes to the examination system, introduced by the Northern Universities Matriculation Board and its new School Certificate examination. Nine of the school's pupils forsook the old Oxford Senior Local Examination in favour of the new, and all passed, whereas of the eight who entered for Oxford, only four passed. This no doubt established a standard for future entrants. The Christmas 1917 edition of the school magazine ended with the reminder that at the time of publication, the Great War had cost the lives of fifteen old boys; one hundred and forty-nine more were on active service, as were six masters.

A common item of conversation in Harrogate during February 1918 was the appearance of a tank, which formed the centrepiece of "Tank Day" during which funds were collected for war loans. The tank trundled up Station Parade, and was exhibited in Library Gardens, with Mayor Johnson standing on top. It doubtless proved a magnet for many of the school's pupils, especially those familiar with Mr. H.G. Well's novel "The Land Ironclads".

An unsavoury but useful item appeared on the town's streets in c.1915, when the swill, or pig bin, was introduced. The idea was that householders would save waste food separately from other household waste, so that it could be fed to pigs. There is evidence that school children were encouraged to assist the process, but by what means, is unsure. Rationing was in force towards the end of the Great War, so it is unlikely that the school's saved waste food contained much meat!

It was at this time that Harrogate Corporation established a separate office of public health a few doors away from the Heywra Crescent building, where citizens could freely obtain large jars of disinfectant. The proximity of this office became significant within a few years, with the global outbreak of a deadly strain of influenza.

At the very beginning of the twentieth century and the outbreak of the South African

War, the political establishment was given much to think about concerning the population's health and welfare. To the shock of many, the average health and general constitution of many enlisted men appeared to be well below the desirable norm. Such concern was probably not the result of a genuine desire to improve the lives of the people, but rather the fighting efficiency and stamina of those fighting the war. After 1914, the same concerns reappeared with a vengeance, and may have played a part in Lloyd George's promotion of a new Education Act, bringing in the distinguished historian H.A.L. Fisher to frame the Bill's principle clauses. The new Act made attendance at school compulsory until the age of fourteen, with no exceptions, and any remaining fees for elementary education were finally abolished. Children between the ages of 14 and 18 were to have the opportunity to attend "day continuation" classes, and the concept of free places for able pupils was enshrined in legislation. At the same time, the welfare of teachers was enhanced by bringing them in to the national scheme for pensions, and also making their salaries uniform throughout the country.

The edition of Midsummer 1918 saw the "Harrogatonian's" editor again bemoaning pupil's unwillingness to part with the two pence needed to purchase the journal, comparing such an attitude with that of Norman Rae of Rossett Green who had given £3,000 to found a scholarship to send pupils to University. The school leaving age at this time was fourteen, but headmaster Thoseby wrote "..*and if parents would realise that the school leaving age for intelligent boys and girls ought to be 18, and not 14 or 15, the Harrogate Secondary School would before long begin to rank with the most distinguished schools in the country"*. At the same time, the governors considered founding a V.C. scholarship to commemorate the "*achievements and patriotic service of the school's old boys."* In fact, the number of scholarships increased throughout the 1920's and 1930's, and between 1919 and 1945, eighteen were awarded to boys and eight to girls.

When the Armistice was signed in November 1918, and the Great War reached its squalid end, the cost to the Harrogate Municipal Secondary School was announced at assembly the same month : twenty one old boys had been killed.

Chapter three

The Jazz age

Even the most imperceptive citizen must have realised that the ending of the Great War was going to introduce a completely new world order, apart, that is, from Harrogate Corporation, who seem to have believed that the clock could be turned back to 1914, so that life could resume its old, comfortable security. In January 1919 the Town Clerk read a letter from the Secretary of U.S. President Wilson, regretting that the President could not break off from the Paris Peace conference to come to Harrogate and be photographed taking tea in the Hotel Majestic. At the same council meeting, Alderman Houfe discussed plans to build "housing for the working classes" on a field in Ripon Road, as part of Lloyd George's drive for "homes for heroes". The town's population in the census of 1921 had grown from the 1911 figure of 33,703 to 38,885, and it was to increase even more during the 1920's, until reaching 43,758 in 1931.These figures are significant, because almost from the time of the 1918 Armistice, it was clear to the authorities that the Secondary Municipal School needed extra accommodation.

From the time the school opened in 1903-4, until December 1910, housing development in Harrogate increased by 27.31%, and during the second decade, by 9.64% The increase in the 1920's was 29.65%, twentieth century Harrogate's biggest increase by decade. Purely in terms of new housing, the time between 1911 and 1920 saw 210 houses built in the locality of King Edward's Drive and Bilton Lane alone, 127 built in High Harrogate, and more throughout the town, The same rate occurred in the 1920's on a much bigger scale, as for example at Knaresborough Road, where 413 homes were built, or the 298 at Oatlands. All this shows that almost from the time it opened, Harrogate's Secondary Municipal School, squeezed awkwardly into the old Technical College, was subject to overcrowding. In the more socially aware world of post-1918, it was not surprising that improvements were soon suggested, improvements made all the more pressing as the ramifications of the 1918 Act became apparent.

The spring of 1919 saw the school's governors pressing the Education Authority to do something about overcrowding at the school, with the result that in May 1919, the architect T.E. Marshall, FRIBA, prepared site plans for a fifteen acre plot of land that measured 685 by 954 feet to the south of Otley Road, part of which allowed for a 45 foot road, later known as Arthur's Avenue. Locally, the site was called Goodrick's field, from butcher Goodrick's habit of keeping livestock there before slaughter. Before the Great War, this had also been where circuses and spectacles had performed, such as Buffalo Bill's Wild West Show. The field was actually part of Blyth Nook farm, once part of the extensive property of M.P. Thomas Collins. On 8th October 1919, the

County Council of the West Riding of Yorkshire approved the purchase of the site for a school, an excellent choice, in view of the healthy and convenient location.

In mid-summer 1919, the school learned of the retirement of its first headmaster, Mr. Watson, who had been running the Technical and Evening schools since stepping aside for Mr. Thoseby. His successor at the "Tech", as it was known, was Mr. R.H. Parker, who in 1921 designed the school's memorial to the old boys who had been killed in the Great War, which included the name of Donald S. Bell, VC, who died in 1916, but not that of Archie White, VC, who died in 1971.

Other magazine gossip included reference to A.A. Thomson, who had been a Lieutenant in the Great War, having seen service in Mesopotamia and France, and who was now reported as working for a well-known London weekly. One sign of the times, with its emphasis on out-door activities, and the rise of the English folk song movement, was the introduction to the school's curriculum of Swedish gymnastics and Morris Dancing, said to have been practised with enthusiasm in the school yard.

The year 1919 was a key one for the staff, in that the addition in September of Miss C.H. Andrews, who obtained her M.A. from Cambridge, and in October of Mr. Thomas H. Lusher, who held an B.Sc. from Durham, added immeasurably to the school's academic and personal excellence. Miss Andrews became senior mistress and senior history mistress, and Mr. Lusher (known affectionately as "Tommy") became senior master and senior mathematics master, also serving as headmaster during the Second World War.

The following year, Mr.J.T. Fairman took over the boys' physical education, and in September 1921, Miss E. Jennings joined the staff of the English Department, which she eventually came to head. These changes occurred at a time when the Education Committee was struggling to solve the school's obvious problems of over-crowding, a difficulty that caused the chairman of the governors, Mr.W. Raworth, much anxiety. Nationally, average classes were large, with totals of more than sixty being the norm in over one quarter of British state schools. The Local Education Authorities still administered education, with half the cost coming from the state. This balance meant, inevitably, that the state would eventually meddle in local education at a rate commensurate to its degree of funding. Yet at the time, this was not necessarily seen as a bad thing.

A temporary remedy for overcrowding occurred in 1920, when Cumberland House in Park View was acquired to provide space for three forms of girls. This was only a couple of minutes' walk from the main building round the corner in Heywra Crescent, and must have provided very pleasant accommodation, as in those days, both Park

View and East Parade overlooked the un-built Sheepshanks' Fields estate. This was an area of agricultural fields and trees that, back in the nineteenth century, Alderman Richard Ellis had earmarked for Harrogate's pleasure gardens. When the estate was developed in the interwar decades, it was however houses, rather than gardens, that were the order of the day.

By 1921, the County Education Committee began to implement their earlier approval of the Marshall plan to build a new educational facility at the Otley Road site. As the 1920's progressed, the need for such a new facility increased, as Harrogate's house building rate of 29.65% made it the twentieth century town's busiest decade for building and expansion, as compared, for example with figures of 8.86% for the 1980's, or 9.19% for the 1990's. On 27th April 1921, the tenant of this part of Blyth Nook Farm, Mr. Thomas Daniel, was served a notice to quit, although in order to keep down the compensation cost, he was allowed to continue to pasture animals until summer's end. A smaller plot of land, more or less opposite the junction of Cold Bath Road, and tenanted by George and Charles Winterburn, was acquired on 17th June, when the Winterburns agreed to vacate their holding. Outright purchase of the whole plot was completed on 20th June 1921, with the indenture being drawn up and signed on 28th June. This indenture paid Thomas Collins' executors, William Henry Gott and Miles Stapylton (acting on behalf of inheritor W.F. Collins), £7,100 for the fifteen acre plot, subject to a few stipulations, such as a prohibition on hanging out washing. One other significant stipulation was (5) that *"the council, their successors or assigns, will fence off the said plot of land conveyed from the adjoining hereditaments and will forever maintain and keep such fences in good repair at their own expense...".* When the purchase was formally approved by the full Education Committee on 26th July, the committee resolved *"that the cost of the site, less one third, being the usual grant to be charged on the townships served by the school".* Eventually, Harrogate Corporation borrowed £4,000 towards the payment of £4,844 that was two thirds of the total cost of purchase. Eventually, Harrogate corporation paid more than £10,000 towards the erection and furnishing of the new school, which was not to be completed until 1933.

More than a decade was to pass before the new school would be ready to receive pupils, and during this time, the surrounding catchment area experienced phenomenal expansion. Harrogate's 29.65% housing growth rate during the 1920's was reflected in the development of Arthur's Avenue from 0 to 12 homes, St. Andrew's Crescent from 0 to 25 homes, and St. Hilda's Road, from 0 to 37 homes. With a total population growth from 38,885 in 1921 to 43,758 in 1931, Harrogate's new Grammar School was not only desirable but essential.

In 1926, the Government published the Hadow Report, which recommended that all children at the age of eleven or twelve years should be transferred to secondary or senior schools and that the leaving age should be fixed at fifteen, an achievement that did not come into force until 1947. A year after the Hadow report's appearance, the County Council's special subcommittee for Secondary Education met at County Hall on 24th May to consider a letter from the governors of the Harrogate Secondary School, who urged the necessity for obtaining the approval of the Board of Education for the commencement of building operations in respect of new premises for Harrogate's Secondary School. It was resolved that the architect (presumably from Marshall's office) proceed with the preparation of revised plans in accordance with the suggestions of the Board of Education. Instead of the separate secondary schools envisaged in 1921 for boys and girls, the revised plan called for a single establishment for both sexes.

Ex pupil R.H. Hebbron provides a clear view of the school in the mid-1920's: *"It was a happy school, and the teaching methods were very much the traditional chalk and talk approach, and although this was mitigated with inspirational teaching, it also enabled less talented teachers to do little other than regurgitate sections of text books. Subjects taught included English, mathematics, physics, chemistry, history, geography, French, Latin, physical exercises, woodwork for boys and domestic science for girls. Religious instruction was provided, but it was somewhat low-key."* Mr. Hebbron recalled *"the masters' room was on the upper floor, and on entering, visitors often had to fight their way through a thick fug of smoke produced by Mr. Jacot's pipe. Jacot was a heavy pipe smoker. He had been a drill master in the First World War, and in the 1920's he drilled the boys in the school yard, often making them stand at knees half-bend till they dropped. He could utter alarming oaths which sounded very effective, but which had quite simple meanings like: thunder in the air!"*

Class teaching was occasionally supplemented by field trips, and one included a trip to the Dales to witness a solar eclipse. Such trips had to be paid for, so pupils with no money could not go. It was at this time that a visit to Belgium was arranged.

The staff in c.1926 included the head, Mr. A.E. Thoseby, who taught Latin and the classics, deputy head "Teddy" Morris, who taught physics, and had a spinal problem caused by a rugby accident, the brilliant and inspirational mathematician, "Tommy" Lusher, English teachers Mr. Pendlebury and "Cush" Cowley, woodwork teacher "Tommy" Kitching, the celebrated geography teacher Mr. Hislop, Latin and history teacher Eric Fisher, and the senior mistress, Miss Everett, who taught English and drama. Ex pupil R.H. Hebbron recalls that Miss Everett mounted several effective plays and tableaux, and that life was difficult for female teachers, as they were not allowed to stay in the profession if they married.

Music teaching was still primitive, with no tuition in theory, sight reading or instrumental performance, the only activity being singing hymns or folk-songs. Sport was divided into football and cricket for the boys, and tennis and hockey for the girls, strict segregation being the norm. Mr. Fairman trained the boys, and Miss Buchanan the girls. The main playing field was at Goodrick's Field, but the Haywra Crescent Building had two smaller play areas, surfaced with tar macadam, including an open shed beneath the gymnasium.

Mr. Hebbron recalls that the school basement was filled with kitchens, a dining room, the wood-work room, and the caretakers department, run by Mr. Fallon, who was known as "Old Pluto", and the "king of the underworld". His opposite number, Mrs. Fallon, cooked the school meals and was known as "Auntie". At break, the children could buy a glass of milk and a biscuit for a few pence, but the main meal of three courses cost one shilling. At Christmas, a special dinner was provided in the basement; this was widely appreciated, and cost one shilling and sixpence.

Three figures who to their ex-pupils still appeared outstanding, nearly eighty years later, were the headmaster, Mr. Thoseby who seemed always to have the appropriate aphorism or Latin quotation at hand, and who was fond of saying "*you must learn to acquire an enquiring mind*" or "*by precept upon precept, line upon line, here a little, there a little – every day*"; the two others being "Tommy" Lusher, the mathematics master, and geography teacher Hislop.

The uniform at this time consisted of a blue cap for boys with an embroidered shield in yellow and the monogram "H.S.S." for "Harrogate Secondary School". The girls wore a blue gym slip, and a coloured hat band. In about 1927 a new comprehensive uniform was introduced, based on the colours brown and red. Boys wore a brown cap with an embroidered red cross, monogram, and shield. Their blazer was brown, and carried an elaborately embroidered coat of arms, with the old Harrogate motto "*Arx Celebris Fontibus*" (a place celebrated for its springs) on the breast pocket. Girls wore a brown blazer similar to that of the boys, a brown gym slip with red girdle, a cream coloured blouse, long brown stockings and knickers, and in summer a cream cotton dress with a faint brown check. In summer, girls wore a panama hat with a brown hat-band. Ties were of red and brown stripes. According to the school magazine, Denton's outfitters in Beulah Street was the main supplier. Ex-pupil Margaret McGeorge recalls that girls were supposed to wear their hats on entering and leaving the school buildings, but stuffed them in their pockets, only wearing them on coming within range of a teacher.

Ex-pupil Ruth Coombes recalls that orphanage children attending the school always had new uniforms, whereas some other children made do with second-hand ones. Mrs. Coombes also recalls that fees were three guineas a term, unless a scholarship had been won, and that she felt privileged to attend *"Harrogate Grammar felt itself a cut above the free council schools and its teachers were university graduates, always gowned in class or assembly. Children always walked to school, and although some came from less affluent backgrounds, none ever looked poor. Harrogate then, as in 2003, was an affluent place, and even when the depression started to bite, the town escaped its worst effects.*

In class, we each had our own wooden desk, with a lift-up lid, and our books were kept inside, so we bought padlocks to keep them secure. Each desk had an inkwell, and by then, many pupils had fountain pens, such as my Conway Stewart. Pupils were also expected to buy their books, which were usually second hand, as well as calculating equipment, protractors, set squares, etc. School began at 9.00am, and finished at 4.00pm. Many students brought sandwiches to eat at lunch, or used the school tuck shop, which included pear drops, and aniseed balls at a penny a portion. Some children such as myself, went home for lunch, and in those days children walked everywhere, even from a young age. Even a little girl on her own felt safe. There were no school buses, although the farming families sent their children by steam train, or by buses, which were reliable.

Most of the female teachers were young, and I especially remember Miss Holmes, because her face had been scarred after a fall into an open fire, Her lively character shone through her horrific injuries, and Miss Holmes enthused each of her charges with a love of Keats, Wordsworth and other great English poets. All the boys took woodwork, but for girls there was a subject called "cookery, laundry and housewifery". This was taught by Miss Wilkins in what today would be a health and safety nightmare: a windowless cellar where you could smell fumes from the adjacent coke-fired boiler. I learnt how to cook a suet pudding and to clean ink off clothes with milk, these being the days before washing machines. The number of pupils in each class numbered about thirty, for whom a variety of extra-curricular activities were available, organized by mostly male teachers who stayed behind after 4.00pm. I especially enjoyed the drama group and the school debating society. We had the usual diet of Shakespeare and Sheridan, as well as modern plays by such playwrights as J.B. Priestley. We enjoyed the end of Christmas term parties, when for once, the boys and girls and staff all mixed together, doing such dances as the waltz, the Valeta, Gay Gordons, Chain dancing, and, best of all, Excuse me dances. Unlike the Council schools, we had no medical care, no eye-testing, and no visits from the dentist or nit-nurse.

I am now in my eighties, and looking back across the years, I am so grateful for that education which stood me in such good stead, for although I left the school at the age of fourteen, the love of learning took hold and is still with me. I remember the respect we pupils had for each other and for the teachers, and the respect that those teachers in turn showed us. Most importantly of all, we learnt to respect ourselves."

Ruth Coombes attended the school from 1930 to 1933, and was therefore present during the move from the old building at Haywra Crescent to the new one at Otley Road, but the above recollections refer principally to the former institution.

During the 1920's, classes were large throughout the country, with one quarter having attendances of sixty pupils. This was at a time when the local authority still administered state education, with half the cost and all of the policy coming from the state. Harrogate's Municipal Secondary School, with its reliance on scholarship winning or fee paying as a means of entry, was not a candidate for all of the state's health measures, although there is evidence to show that sporadic attention was paid to pupil's health. In July 1923 a visiting lecturer asked junior children to *"clean their teeth every night for at least a month"*; what happened when the month ended is not clear! Meanwhile, the school's sporting prowess increased during the 1920's. By 1925, the school magazine was reporting that the cricket first eleven had won six out of eight matches, the football team had won twenty-four out of twenty-six matches, and the hockey team had won seventeen out of eighteen. These were encouraging results. Instruction in swimming was also provided, and ex-pupil Ruth Coombes recalls that girls and boys were taken to swim at the Dragon Parade baths, although the school never allowed mixed bathing. Mrs Coombes recalled that the girl's sports mistress *"...Miss Buchanan gave stirling service to scores of scared youngsters like me, whom she taught to swim with confidence; we were therefore heartbroken when she died at the age of 32 from pneumonia, a disease which today (i.e.2003) would be so readily treatable with antibiotics"*. Following Miss Buchanan's death on 22nd February 1933, Miss T. Duckworth was appointed as her replacement.

The later 1920's saw moves in Parliament to frame a new Education Bill, which sought – among other things – to raise the school leaving age to fifteen, and also to reform provision for the teaching of religion. This caused difficulties with Roman Catholics on the labour back-benches. It was however the House of Lords who threw out the Bill, and it was not until the Act of 1936 that provision was made for the school leaving age to be raised to fifteen, although the implementation of this provision by September 1939 was deferred until 1947.

Harrogate, in the 1920's, gave much attention to extending and improving its Spa facilities, a policy that made sound economic sense. By the time of the calamitous depression following the Wall Street crash of 1929, the British Spa Federation advised Alderman Barber that Harrogate's spa-based economy was creating more income than that of the town's six British rivals combined. However, the outlook was not good, and one of the motivations of those who sought to diversify the town's economy was the strengthening of local employment and the creation of alternative sources of income. This is why within only four years of the publication in November 1928 of Alderman Barber's plans for the construction of a huge "Spa Forum" in Low Harrogate's Crescent Gardens, Councillor Harry Bolland was calling for Harrogate to have "*one of the biggest conference halls in England*". However, it was clear that no matter how many improvements were made to the Spa, even with the construction of a large conference centre, that Harrogate could not absorb all of the Municipal Secondary School's leavers, which in 1930 had 530 pupils. Consequently, the majority of school leavers would have fixed their sight on gaining employment beyond Harrogate's boundary.

The House of Lords 1931 rejection of the new Education Bill occurred the same year as the Harrogate Municipal Secondary School changed its title to that of Harrogate Grammar School, and the uniform switched from blue and gold to red and brown. The change of name reflected the feelings of the governors, who, by this time, knew that the opening of their splendid new building on Otley Road was only a matter of time, and that they would soon be well placed to meet the highest aspirations of their catchment area

The Harrogate Advertiser for 16th September 1933 contains a report of an "Old Students' reunion", held at the Grand Hotel in Cornwall Road, in celebration of "*the coming opening of the new Grammar School*". The dinner-dance had been arranged by the "Harrogate Grammar School Old Students' Association" and those present included the headmaster, Mr. A.E. Thoseby, the Mayor and Mayoress of Harrogate, Alderman and Mrs. Whiteoak, the Director of Education, Mr. W. Jalland, and several distinguished old boys, including author A.A. Thomson and Olympic Games rower T.H. Tyler. A presentation was made to Edwin Morris, the retiring senior master, who was given a writing desk and chair, and the chairman of the governors spoke of the new building as being "*all that the heart could desire. It was spacious, nobly proportioned, well decorated and ventilated, and splendidly equipped*".

The foregoing words make clear that the Grammar School was not ready for opening at the beginning of the Autumn term, the reason for the delay being the indisposition of the Princess Royal, following an operation for appendicitis. Harrogate, during the interwar years, and especially during the 1920's, had something of an obsession with the Princess Royal, who, as the only daughter of King George V and Queen Mary, was regarded with feelings approaching reverence. The fact that following her wedding in 1922, she and her husband (a future Earl of Harewood) moved into nearby Goldsborough Hall, was not lost on those in socially aware Harrogate who valued having such a celebrity in their midst. An example of the Princess Royal's celebrity in Harrogate can be seen by examining copies of the "Ackrill Annual", in that between

1922 and 1929, no less than four editions featured the Princess on their front covers. It is therefore understandable that the princess should have been asked to open the Grammar School in September, and equally understandable why, when news of her inability to comply reached the governors, they preferred to put off the opening until November 1933 when the Princess was expected to be available. However, when the Princess was unable to attend in November, the idea of having an official opening seems to have been quietly dropped. The new Harrogate Grammar School opened its doors to pupils on Thursday 7th September 1933, having taken several years to build.

The new school was a nobly proportioned stone built "H" structure containing two quadrangles, one of which was open on one side, as if allowing for future expansion. The sloping nature of the site meant that the section nearest to Otley Road had a ground floor that became a basement as one progressed further away from Otley Road. The main entrance on Arthur's Avenue was given a recessed classical portico in a modified ionic order, and it was a pity that the architect had not the confidence or backing to provide a free-standing colonnade. Had he seen the building, Osbert Lancaster might have described it as "Queen Ann Luftwaffe", which would have been no criticism, as the marriage of English eclecticism to German regularity had produced a handsome building. The façade's design is of a type that was more commonly executed in brick, and the use of grey stone gives a certain cold monumentality to what in dull red brick would have been more immediately appealing, especially with the spacious arched windows. Despite the crassly insensitive additions of seventy years later, it is still possible to capture something of the building's original grandeur.

With its provision for good ventilation, and natural lighting, the new building incorporated concepts that were typical of the period, as for example features that were then being integrated into contemporary hospitals and sanitoria. Indeed, some features were a little too free with fresh air, as the open corridors on the school's south side had to be enclosed after they became blocked with snow! One feature singled out for special comment by the press was that the school possessed "*drying rooms for clothes that get wet*", presumably in the course of rain, or sporting activities.

Arthur's Avenue, which received its first dozen houses only in the later 1920's, probably got its unusual name from an upsurge of public interest in Harrogate's distant past, an interest that had been stimulated by the appearance in 1922 of Walter Kaye's splendid book "Records of Harrogate". Historian William Grainge had previously drawn attention to the antiquities of Harlow Hill, alluding to local "murmurs" of a battle between King Arthur's father, Uther Pendragon, and the Saxon horde. The locality had even boasted a "Pendragon's Cottage" claimed Grainge, and a Windsor Cottage stood on the site of the future junction of Arthur's Avenue when the land was purchased in 1921. At a time of Arthurian populism, it was almost inevitable that a site associated with the national hero, no matter how precariously, should receive his name. It is worth emphasising that Arthur's venue owes its existence to the building of the Grammar School, and not the other way round.

Chapter four

The impact of H. R. C. Carr, 1933-to 1939

When seen for the first time, the new school made a favourable impression on the majority of visitors. Ex-pupil Norman Lusher recalls that he had explored the building even before it opened, crawling beneath the newly laid floor boards and feeling quite awed by the building's splendid dimensions and fittings. By 1933, the authority was only too aware of the great depression's effect on society, so that the Harrogate Herald felt it expedient to explain that "...*the West Riding County Council sanctioned (the) erection of the school before the present economy programme began.*" Harrogate Council had, itself, been obliged to enforce rigid economies, cancelling, for example, the proposal to extend the Royal Baths up Parliament Street as far as the Ginnel.

With a planned capacity for 800 pupils, the new school buildings received 258 boys and 269 girls, a total of 527 pupils. The impression the new school made on these children appeared to match that of Norman Lusher: ex.-pupil Mrs. Ruth Coombes recalls *"the facilities were brand-new and seemed wonderful. There was a lovely dinning room in what is now the school library, better laboratories and lighter and brighter classrooms"*. Ex-pupil Mr. D.S. Bell recalls how impressed he was by the school's size and quality, especially as he had moved from the much smaller Victorian elementary Christ Church School in Church Square. *"The parquet floors looked impressive, as did the indoor loos and the special rooms for such subjects as art, metalwork or gymnastics"*. Mr. Bell's point about the loos is shared by many other members of his, and similar generations, as it used to be common practice to construct such amenities detached from the main school building.

The staff of the old Harrogate Grammar School transferred from Haywra Crescent to Otley Road with comparative ease, and if any bemoaned the loss of the convenient town centre site, they kept their reservations to themselves, in view of the new building's undoubted qualities. The headmaster, Mr. Thoseby, one of whose nicknames was "Tus", was said to be a good disciplinarian, especially regarding mass behaviour. A school magazine later reported an incident at school assembly when coughing was abnormally intrusive, at which Mr. Thoseby reproved the gathering, saying that the coughing must cease, as it was *"not only irreverent, but disrespectful to me"*. Teddy Morris, the deputy, was serving his final year of office during the move to the new school, and indeed his contribution was honoured at the Grand Hotel reunion in September 1933. Another important staff member, Tommy Lusher was widely respected, not only for his brilliant abilities as a teacher of mathematics, but for his self-control, and more will be recorded of this genuinely inspirational figure in the chapter on the Second World War. Miss Andrews, Mr. Kitching, Miss Jennings, Mr.

Fisher, Miss Holmes, Mr. Thompson, Miss Duckworth, and the notorious Jacot were also teaching at this time, as was the diminutive Mr. E.N. Jones, who joined the staff in 1931, soon followed by a new teacher of a new subject, the mechanics master Mr. Beveridge.

Grammar School pupils came from Harrogate town, whose population in 1931 had been put at 43,758, as well as the surrounding country, including such places as Pateley Bridge, Hampsthwaite, Killinghall and Wetherby. The communities in which the majority of these pupils lived, were experiencing the effects (though perhaps not the extreme hardship) of the great depression. It is therefore easy to see that the school's continuing emphasis on such essential occupations as woodwork or mechanics, was encouraged by the state of the employment market in the post-school world in which all pupils would soon find themselves.

As for Harrogate, the 1930's saw a continuation of the extraordinary urbanization that had been such a feature of the 1920's, with a net housing growth rate of 24.03%. The so-called "Saints" development between Oatlands Drive and Wetherby Road was typical, and was within easy walking distance of the Grammar School. The Spa economy of Harrogate continued to make a profit throughout the 1930's, unlike that of just about every other British Spa, but margins were narrow. When the new Grammar School opened, the town was about to embark on the biggest row of its history, occasioned by massive public opposition to the council-built flower beds on West Park Stray, which were removed only in 1934 when the public got rid of the Council. On a more progressive note, the new Sun Pavilion and Colonnade were opened by Lord Horder at Whitsuntide 1933, thus providing a valuable link between the Royal Bath Hospital and Royal Pump Room. Both the Sun Colonnade and Pavilion possessed large areas of removable glazing, to facilitate good ventilation, a feature they shared with the Grammar School.

Something of the time's sombre atmosphere crept into the school magazine in March 1934, "*And so we sit back and let our thoughts wander over the school's past. It cannot be said to have been an uneventful past. Thirty years – of peace, prosperity, of gathering clouds, of war in its most ghastly form, of trade depression in which an entirely new generation has sprung up, a generation brought up in a badly wounded world, which knows little or nothing of a world devoid of unrest and suspicion.*"

For nearly a year, headmaster Thoseby presided over what must have seemed the promised land, but in the early summer of 1934, he announced his retirement to Scarborough. He had been with the school since its inception in 1903, serving at first under Mr. Watson, before becoming Head in 1910. Miss Wade, the needlework mistress since 1903, also announced her resignation. Changes were afoot.

The newly appointed headmaster, Mr. H.R.C. Carr, was an experienced historian with a naval background. After serving with the Royal Marines during the First World War, he resumed modern history at Pembroke College, Oxford, and became senior history master at Alleyn's School, and then headmaster at Queen Elizabeth's Grammar School at Penrith. In 1934, he was appointed successor to Mr. Thoseby at Harrogate Grammar School, with its 630 pupils.

In his first contribution to the school magazine, Mr. Carr indulged one of his hobby horses, noting that *"there is a growing feeling among those interested in education that modern schools concentrate too much on mental and too little on physical development. Accordingly... a short period has been set aside every morning for physical exercises"*. The exercises were, of course strictly segregated, in accordance with society's wishes, for this was at a time when even the entrances to the new Labour Exchange in East Parade were marked separately for men and women, as were the Grammar School's staff rooms.

Within a few months, the town was following Mr. Carr's innovations with interest. In 1935, a state run National Health Service lay over ten years, and a World War, in the future. The old Infirmary in Avenue Road, built back in the 1870's when Harrogate's population was little over 8,000, was clearly inadequate for an enlarged urban area that by 1931 was home to 43,758 adults. In 1932, six years after she had laid the foundation stone, the new hospital on Knaresborough Road was opened by the Princess Royal, so it was understandable that the hospital and the Grammar School felt a certain kinship. Consequently, the school established a "Harrogate Grammar School Hospital Cot," which was maintained by monthly school collections, and from profits resulting from the sales of chocolates and biscuits at the morning interval "school shops".

The new term in September 1935 witnessed a change of emphasis, not with the curriculum, but with the manner of its enforcement. The introduction of a range of commercial subjects had been an understandable move, given the employment reality facing school leavers, and the fact that Harrogate Grammar School was not run by the governors as an academic forcing house. Commercial studies included shorthand, typing, and book-keeping, all very valuable skills, for which a regular demand existed in the retail markets of northern England. The school knew that it had a responsibility for all its pupils, not merely the academically advanced, and consequently regulated the curriculum in consultation with the local education authority, rather than by order of central government. However, the school appears to have practiced the policy of shunting weaker pupils into the area of commercial studies, thus giving it a lower status. This was deplorable, and just another face of the bad old English attitude to "trade", that had caused the country to be eclipsed in certain areas by both Germany and the USA. Indeed, the inspectors criticized this aspect of the Grammar School's administration in the 1937 inspection, pointing out that as the two commercial studies "remove" forms (C and D) took approximately half of all the pupils in the school, the proportion of children associated with a lower status aspect of the curriculum was very high. During the 1935-1936 year, the school had 321 boys and 335 girls, whose total of 656 gives some indication of the extent of the problem.

One of the best aspects of the Grammar School at this period was the importance accorded to sport and extra-curricular activities, and for this humanistic approach, much credit belongs with Mr. Carr, who encouraged the expansion of association football, cricket, hockey and tennis. Mr. Carr's own hobby of mountaineering led to the growth of climbing, hiking and walking by pupils, and some of the most personal photographic mementos of these times record various outings under his supervision. Other staff were able to influence the nature and direction of extra-curricular activities, and when the distinguished artist Oliver Pemsel took charge of the school's art department, visits to galleries and museums were undertaken. It was probably Mr. Pemsel's influence that was responsible for the *Harrogatonian* printing several fine woodcuts in various editions throughout the 1930's, a practice that was revived for a short time in the school magazine of the mid-1980's. Examples of Oliver Pemsel's work were later held in Harrogate's Mercer Art gallery.

Mr. Hislop the geography master, encouraged field trips, and one group of pupils visited a school in France. Commenting on the experience, a pupil wrote that *"... the French boys would seem noisy, gay, and talkative to you, and if you learnt German here you would have the pleasure of greeting your German master with outstretched arm and a Heil Hitler, which is having a great vogue at the moment."*

The Grammar School possessed a League of Nations union, and if pupils had an understanding of the darkening international situation, it does not seem to have impinged on their lessons, as several ex-pupils have recalled that the history curriculum contained almost nothing of import after the death of Queen Victoria, and certainly nothing of a contemporary nature. Any information about events in Europe seem to have been given on a one-to-one basis.

One former pupil gained the impression that the teaching staff did not have a uniform approach to the threat from Europe, and recalls that whereas Mr.Carr seemed at times to be pessimistic, Mr Lusher possessed an unshakeable faith in the country's ability to weather the coming storm. Others retained different memories of their teachers, and Fred Roberts, who attended from 1933 to 1940, remembers his occasional disappointment with the quality of some of the instruction, a point emphasized in the 1937 Board of Education inspection. Mr. Roberts' description of some of the instruction he received, is so perceptive as to be worth recounting in detail : *"Perhaps my biggest disappointment was the failure of the school to provide sound teaching in chemistry and physics. There was a shortage of well-trained teachers at secondary level during the years following World War One, and this showed up in the quality of the science teaching at Harrogate Grammar School. Mr. "Piggy" Wheeler was the main physics teacher and the poor fellow was perpetually struggling to cope with his damaged lungs which caused him to go "a-hum, a-hum" every few seconds. In many lessons we simply had to copy out extracts from an old-fashioned book by Gregory and Hadley; the illustrations were like old engravings and whenever a source of light appeared in the chapter on optics it was a candle flame! For a year or two there was an elderly fellow on the staff called Geikie who had no idea whatsoever of how to teach physics; we boys decided that he suffered badly from piles, or why otherwise would he walk along the school corridors perpetually scratching his bottom? I find it hard to remember many experiments being demonstrated on the laboratory bench by either of these men and rarely were we allowed to perform experiments by ourselves. If I had ever entertained the idea of becoming a Physicist it had certainly gone for good by the time I was through middle school. If Mr. "Peg-Leg" Peters, with his Bsc. Honours Physics from Sheffield had not turned up in time* (note: Mr. Peters joined the staff in 1936), *I doubt whether I would have got pass in physics...But the greatest disappointment for me was in the chemistry teaching of Mr.Willie Wallis...in charge here throughout my seven years at the school. He always looked grey and ill, in fact it was said that he suffered from chronic insomnia, which probably gave him the strained look about the eyes and the perpetual scowl. I can see him now, standing behind the teacher's bench in the junior chemistry laboratory, peering round the class to find a boy who was not paying attention and meanwhile jerking his shoulders in order to draw his frayed shirt cuffs out of sight. When he did find his culprit, he told him he was wasting an important opportunity in life, a chance to learn chemistry. Then we all had to listen to the old, old story, which always began : "a man came to me last night to ask me to teach his son some chemistry..." the rest was to the effect that if this lad had concentrated in school when he had had the chance to learn, etc.... By now we had wasted twenty minutes or so, and as I had decided to become a chemist I was inwardly fuming. Finally he would sigh, strike a light and light a Bunsen burner"* Mr. Roberts goes on to recall that it was probably his own cramming at home with Holmyards's "Inorganic Chemistry" that got him the desired pass.

With reference to his non-scientific education, Mr. Roberts recalls that "*I always enjoyed geography and art and had no difficulty with maths and English. But I did have to struggle with French and Latin which I found dull and uninteresting. The French teacher, Monsieur Jacot, tried to produce results from the class by frightening the living daylights out of us, whereas S.A.M. Male, with his Oxbridge degree in classics, failed to interest the class in Latin and had no idea of how to teach the subject or even keep us in order.*(Note: Mr. Male was a member of staff between 1936 and

1946) *The latter comments could be applied to Miss Holmes' attempts to teach us her subject, scripture. Although I had no difficulty in learning enough history to get good exam marks, I did find it difficult to become interested in the machinations of British kings and queens etc...Our teacher, Mr. "Chips" Fisher, was a good teacher, and a good effortless disciplinarian. We respected him for his interest in his subject acting as recorder for the Yorkshire Archaeological Society. Under "Chips" guidance we set up an informal group to visit sites of historical importance within cycling distance of Harrogate. I remember a day at York; our group had gone twenty miles, and was approaching the outer suburbs, when "Chips" buzzed up on his two-stroke. After "doing the Minster and part of the city walls" we were left alone to eat our sandwiches, speculating that he had gone to a pub for a pint and a pipe, but he eventually returned and we headed off towards Clifford's Tower...Finally, mention must be made of two further items in the curriculum – woodwork and metalwork. We had a double-period a week for two years under the close supervision of Mr. "Tommy" Kitching, who was likely to blow his top and go red in the face if he caught a lad using a tool in such a way that he was likely to injure himself. Then for a third year we went to the metal working shop where, under the efficient though calmer direction of "Sandy" Beveridge [left 1935], we learnt how to shape and solder tinplate, use hacksaws, files and power drills on metal plate and even have a go at turning on a lathe. These practical subjects were not taken up to school certificate level, but the experience with tools thus gained proved useful during adult life..."*

Over four days in early May 1937, the school was subjected to a further inspection by the Board of Education. Since the last inspection, in 1925, the Grammar School had changed its name, its address, its uniforms, and had moved away from a post-war world into a pre-war one. It had 324 boys and 339 girls, who were still segregated, not only having separate school entrances, but playing fields that were divided down the middle by a thick hedge! The preamble to the 1937 report noted that since the last inspection, the number of pupils had increased by fifty percent, rising from 407 to 663, and that their average leaving age was sixteen years and four months for boys and sixteen years seven months for girls. The inspectors noted the unusually small number of pupils in the sixth form, a fact put down to the school's location in an area of easy local employment, in which 7.5% of all pupils in the 11 to 16 age group were in the sixth form, compared with the national average of 16.8%. This small sixth form was therefore not managing to send many students to University or training college, and from 1932 to 1936 inclusive, only seventeen pupils were entered.

The inspectors noticed that the increased attention given to sport and physical training meant that the showers, installed only in 1933, were no longer adequate, in that they *"no longer conform with modern requirements"*. The inspectors made no reference to the lack of a swimming pool, and summed up the physical training for boys as *"good"* whereas for girls it was *"poor"*.

It was with the curriculum that the most considered criticisms were apparent, particularly in the final stages: *"the curriculum, especially in the first three years, is in many respects wide and generous"* and *"the present policy is not to grade pupils in the first three years, so as to avoid making some forms contain only backward pupils"*. At this period, streaming was introduced only in the fourth year.

Other comments were more specific: *"It is very doubtful whether it is advisable for all pupils to start Latin, seeing that so many will drop the subject in two years"* and *"the provision for music is poor"*; clearly, the days of a good school orchestra were well into the future. In their summary, the inspectors noted that *"there is good teaching in several subjects, but the general standard of work cannot be called high"*. The only "good" subjects were geography, and (inevitably) mathematics.

As for the staff, the inspectors considered them to be *"in general, a hardworking and conscientious body...but...cannot be called outstanding... some members have trouble in the matter of discipline.."* reading between the lines, and in the light of comments later made by ex-pupils, it is possible that the inspectors found a number of outstanding talents, who "carried" a certain amount of "dead wood", a situation that was hardly Mr. Carr's fault, in that he had been appointed only three years previously, and unlike the managers of Harrogate's Grand or Majestic hotels, was without the power to carry out mass sackings that might have improved matters.

The complaint, already made by ex-pupil Fred Roberts, about the habit of copying chunks from often redundant textbooks, was also highlighted by the school inspectors, who urged the discontinuation of dictated or copied notes, and their replacement by notes taken by pupils during their lessons. Interestingly, in view of prevalent social trends, the inspectors recommended that although Harrogate Grammar School *"put boys and girls in separate forms for the first three years, there are many who would prefer the boys and girls to be mixed at as young an age as possible"*.

The school's new hand-press and acquisition of a quantity of type was praised, as was the production of a good quality school magazine, and the inspectors also noted the system of dental inspection recently introduced by the authority. In conclusion, the report stated that *"the school is passing through a difficult phase...the general standard of work has not kept apace with the increased number of pupils...the curriculum is in general planned on broadminded and modern lines...and.... commercial courses need improving"*

The same year that the above report appeared, 1937, also saw Harrogate experiencing significant changes to its face: the council prepared a plan for the replacement of much of the town's sub-standard housing, the town centre received a new cinema next to St. Peter's Church, the Market Hall was destroyed by fire on 31st January, and on 6th October, the Minister of Health laid the foundation stone of a large extension to the Royal Baths, months after the Victorian Wintergarden was wrecked. Within two more years, the Spa Rooms, arguably the best building in the town, was over-hastily demolished.

When the authors of the 1937 inspection reported on the Grammar School's arts department, they made favourable allusion to the hand-press and type available to the staff and pupils, the most immediate result of which was the appearance of the "Harrogatonian", enriched by a series of first rate wood and lino cuts and drawings. This was certainly the brainchild of Oliver Pemsel, the school's distinguished art master, who also added to the cover the motto *"Arx Celebris Fontibus"*, which was Harrogate's motto: "A Citadel (or place) famed for its springs".

The intake of new pupils rose to a record 666 in the Autumn of 1937, and it was only a year previously that the West Riding County Council purchased two parcels of land to the south of the school, from the Y.M.C.A.'s trustees, Bain, Watson and Ogden. The new purchase brought the playing fields to a total of thirteen acres of ground, and would afford future opportunities to extend either sporting facilities or buildings. The school magazine explained that before the new land could be utilized, it would have to be levelled. Other news was that sixty rose trees had been planted in the south quadrangle; the school tuck shop, established two years earlier, was showing a profit of little over £20 per annum, and a shelter had been built for the cars of staff. One of the adverse criticisms of the recent inspection, levelled against the school's music instruction, was answered in part by a note that Margaret Plummer had won distinction in music, and *"we hope she will win a scholarship at the Royal College of Music"*. Finally, the school was reported as having visited Harrogate Theatre on 7th June to watch a performance of A.A. Thomson's play "Lilac Lady"

The decline of the school's branch of the League of Nations may have had much to do with disillusion with that body in the light of their inability to stand up to the dictators, and in the summer of 1937, the Harrogate Grammar School branch was discontinued. At the same time, perhaps in dawning realisation that war was coming, steps were being taken by Squadron-Leader W.S. Harms to establish what later became the number fifty-eight Air Cadet Corps in Harrogate, based at the Grammar School. The squadron had to be self-supporting, and was allowed registration as a member of the corps only when sufficient money had been raised by voluntary means.

This, then, was 1937, in many ways a key year for the school, and whatever memories ex-pupils may have had for the many and varied activities they experienced during that year, the majority, if asked, would probably place one particular event above all others in the hierarchy of their memories: the procession to mark the 1937 Coronation of King George VI. In May 1937, Harrogate Corporation planned several events of a patriotic and celebratory nature to mark the Coronation, including a procession of hundreds of decorated floats entered by groups as diverse as local friendly societies and traders. One such float was reserved for Harrogate Grammar School. When the day of the parade came, the weather was foul, with light wind and torrential down-pourings of rain. Harrogate Grammar School had designed a symbolic ship to represent the ship of state; it was captained by Lord Nelson, and bore Britannia enthroned beneath a canopy, accompanied by sea-nymphs and mermaids with a crew of suitably attired ratings. The whole enormous conception had been built at the Grammar School, and assembled at New Park power station, from whence it was intended to join the parade round the town and up Parliament Street. Almost within moments of setting off, disaster struck, when the mast of the ship of state became entangled in overhead power lines, which could have electrocuted the sea-nymphs and ratings, and plunged the town into darkness. However, the procession continued, minus the crow's nest, and accompanied by merciless rain, that drenched the participants and spectators, turning the fair on south Stray into a quagmire. It came as no surprise when the next edition of the school magazine gave only passing notice to the defunct ship of state.

In 1938, the Spens report on secondary education appeared, which said that there should be a tri-partite system of secondary education, and that all secondary education should be free. The introduction of the eleven-plus examination was a natural corollary to the system. However, the Second World War prevented the report's implementation.

On 6th February 1939, the Mayor of Harrogate, Councillor H. Dawson and Dr. J.L. Wesley-Smith led a meeting in the Council chamber to promote the idea of an air corps squadron to be based at Harrogate Grammar School. The outcome was that an anonymous gentleman agreed to cover all the expenses, and a committee was formed, (including the headmaster Mr. Carr) under the chairmanship of Mr. G.A. Holmes, who sustained the squadron for seven years. The "Harrogatonian" for summer 1939 reported that the West Riding authority had granted the use of the Grammar School's buildings as headquarters for the Harrogate no.58 squadron of the A.D.C.C. which had been formed in March 1939. The corps purpose was to *provide cadets with elementary training so that they may supplement the R.A.F. in time of war.*

The death, in British Columbia, of the school's first headmaster, Mr. Watson, was reported in April 1939. He was eighty-six when he died, and his headship was, rather unkindly, described as "an accident", in that he had been head of the Technical Institute and Teachers' Centre when the new Secondary School had been established in the same building in 1903. The obituary in the school magazine noted that when head, Mr. Watson had prevented "the separation of the practical from the aesthetic that was so much deplored in the curricular of many secondary schools". Clearly, Mr. Watson had not been a believer in the school as an academic sausage factory.

The Harrogatonian for Summer 1939 reported that in the Autumn term for 1938, Harrogate Grammar School contained 314 boys and 306 girls, the pass rate for the school certificate being eighty percent. The start of the 1939 Autumn term, only a few weeks after the Lord Mayor of London opened the new extension to the Royal Baths, coincided with the outbreak of the Second World War, which began a period of profound change for the school.

Chapter five

The great days of "Tommy" Lusher

At quite an early stage of the War, Harrogate Grammar school discovered that not all threats and dangers came from enemy activity. An outbreak of polio presented the authorities with a dire danger, that actually afflicted several pupils as well as other Harrogate residents. Ex-pupil Gordon Town recalled that at the time of the polio outbreak, children were required to gargle with a solution of potassium permanganate, and that shirkers were identifiable by their lack of purple stained mouths.

Some ex-pupils came to hold the interesting opinion that because Harrogate Grammar School's prefectorial system was so much less formal or rigorous than those of corresponding systems in the south of England, the discipline was correspondingly looser. Without the back-up of zealous prefects, the hard-pressed staff lacked the support necessary for maintaining a tight discipline. Whatever the rights or wrongs of this opinion, nobody can deny that in the Autumn of 1939, and succeeding terms, the staff structure at Harrogate Grammar School was very hard-pressed, if only because most of the younger male staff went off to the war. Ex-pupil Henrik Murden later recalled that *"there were more lady teachers during the war because male teachers were away fighting"*.

In 1939, Harrogate experienced more immediate change than it had done in 1914. The Spa visitors disappeared almost overnight, and the hotels were requisitioned by the government for the war effort, partly because of the wide-spread view that London and its ministries would be bombed. Departments of the Army, Air Force, Pensions Division, Ministry of Supply and others, appeared in the town, along with evacuated civil servants and children, some of whom were sent to the Grammar School, along with children from schools commandeered by the forces. Ashville, for example, was requisitioned by the Air Ministry, causing the school to decamp to Bownes-on-Windermere, and a photograph (see p.75) of a Harrogate Grammar School class at this time shows the youthful Alistair Burnett standing at the back clad in his Ashville blazer. Henrik Murden, son of a civil servant moved to Harrogate, recalled that new pupils were subjected to an "induction" by their school mates, but that in the event, the "induction" ritual was not as bad as it had been painted. Ex-pupil George Holmes also remembered that pupils who had been evacuated to Harrogate appeared to integrate well at the Grammar School, a memory shared by another ex-pupil, Mrs.Jean Barnstead, who recalled *"the arrival at school of an influx of refugees from the continent escaping deportations. Some of them had initial language difficulties but quickly became welcome additions to our school roll"*.

Headmaster Carr joined the R.A.F, serving from 1940 to 1944, and maths teacher Henry Hall joined the army. Some ex-pupils have recorded the opinion that Mr. Carr had been generally pessimistic about the international situation, and was rumoured to have sent his family to Canada before the War, unlike his replacement, senior master Tommy Lusher who apparently never doubted the nation's ability to win through. Although known as "acting head", Mr. Lusher deserved the full title of headmaster, for his tireless work in keeping the school afloat during the difficult war years. Born in South Shields, Mr. Lusher had served in the Army during the First World War, and joined the staff of Harrogate's Secondary Municipal School in 1919; he possessed an astonishing ability for mathematics, winning the prestigious King's Award. Quite apart from his mathematical knowledge, Mr. Lusher was gifted with an ability to communicate, at which art he was reported as being inspirational. His son, Norman, who was a pupil at the school during these years, recalls that when his Father entered a class room, *"all the children were spellbound, as, quite exceptionally, he had the ability to start to write on the blackboard with his left hand, and finish the sentence with his right hand."*

Known as "Tommy", T.H.Lusher was said to possess a fine sense of humour and wonderful self control. His personality has been described as "charismatic" and he was never known to have handed out a single detention, nor of missing a day through illness, a remarkable record for any teacher. The register of staff absences between 1924 and 1949 shows that whereas dozens of other members of staff were away frequently, with a variety of illnesses, Mr. Lusher only had two and a half days absence, and then on official business to Scarborough, Wakefield and London, an incredible record. An example of his humour came with his quip on hearing of the precedence of Lord Beaverbrook's Daily Express over Lord Rothermere's Daily Mail *"It looks as if the mere has merged into the brook"*. Such was the man who became head in 1940.

The teaching body, as has already been noticed, experienced great change at this time, to the unsettlement of the pupils. Former pupil Mr. D.S. Bell [nephew of the V.C. winner] recalled that there was also a change of behaviour with some of the established staff, as, for example, with the popular Mr. Jones, who, before the war, extolled everything German, and had a German wife, but who became more circumspect after the outbreak of war in 1939. There was also Mr. J.D.L. Elliot, the metalwork master, who joined the staff in 1938, and was rumoured to be a "conchie" (conscientious objector), and other ex-pupils have recalled that it was not unusual for boys whose fathers were in the services to shout across the room to one another with accounts of their parent's bravery and sacrifice, in order to discomfort Mr. Elliot!

Physical changes to the Grammar School included the construction of bomb blast walls in some of the corridors, windows taped to reduce splintering, using a horrible-smelling fish glue, and black out regulations. The bomb-blast walls were considered unfair by pupils, as they enabled headmaster Tommy Lusher, his gown billowing, to sweep down unseen on erring pupils.

Air raid precautions were taken very seriously, with barriers of earth erected on the school playing fields, described by ex-pupil Barrie Heads as *"shallow, round semi-trenches"*. Just how effective a protection these primitive earth constructions would have been during an attack on the school, is another matter, but at least the making of them provided the feeling that "steps were being taken". For a short while there were trial evacuations into these "foxholes", but thanks to the natural dampness of Harrogate, and the effects of a Yorkshire winter, their use was abandoned well before the end of the war. Even before the start of the war, preparations for the national emergency were well in hand, and one of Hugh Sykes' first memories of starting at the school in September 1939 was of filling sandbags.

Everybody at Harrogate Grammar School had to carry a gas mask, as there was widespread fear of gas attacks, which fortunately never occurred. For the rest, pupils and staff had exactly the same kind of pressures and worries experienced by later generations: examinations, peer group pressures, economic considerations, reconciling the natural exuberance of youth with the need to respect school discipline, personal difficulties with home and family, and the general trials of life. However, the war-time generation had in addition to deal with the knowledge that someone close might be killed or maimed, their home bombed, their country invaded, or their person harmed. Ex-pupil Mrs. M.R. Barker recalled her feelings on learning of the death of two RAF men who had once been her fellow pupils. People had to cope with rationing of food, which banished such things as oranges or bananas into the realm of history. Clothing often became a matter of "making do and mend", and accepting without comment the cast-off and sometimes shabby garments of others. Power was rationed, often requiring the re-use of dirty bath water, shared cooking facilities, and whole groups of people crowding round a single radio set. The black-out of buildings, to deter aerial attacks, led to many an embarrassing or bruising experience, missed appointments, and general extension of travel time. Yet not everything was in short supply, for as several ex-pupils later recalled, they always had books to study and paper for writing. The Grammar School's railings, on the Otley Road and Arthur's Avenue boundary walls, disappeared to fill the maw of the scrap metal drive, more as a piece of home-front propaganda than as a vital contribution towards the armaments campaign.

Other war-time activities included the formation of a Girls' Air Training Corps, and the recruiting of volunteers for overnight fire watching. War bonds were made available for sale, and funds were raised for the war effort by means of such things as dances for fifth and sixth formers. To music provided by gramophone records, pupils danced the Palais-glide, the Valetta, and enjoyed such tunes as "Blaze Away" and "Poor little Angeline".

Some older pupils were given responsibility for younger children during air raid practise, and it was arranged that in the event of an air raid, groups of children would gather at a central point, from where they would be taken by an older pupil to nearby houses for refuge. Ex-pupil Hugh Sykes recalls that during some trial evacuations to a private house in West End Avenue, he was given glasses of home-made wine by the lady of the house, although he was only fourteen.

The A.R.P. (Air Raid Precautions) took over the main school gymnasium at the start of the war, requiring the school's indoor physical education to take place in the assembly hall. When pupil Donald S. Bell left school in 1940, he served the first part of the "phoney" war as an A.R.P. messenger, waiting for action at the Skipton Road swimming baths, where on several occasions he had to spend the night. Others, still at school, volunteered for fire watch service, and ex-pupil Mrs. Jean Barnstead remembers standing on the roof of the boys' gym watching with horror the fires of Hull during a big air raid.

Beyond the Cricket pavilion, to the east of the school, a hedge divided the playing fields that were close to the school, from the more distant tennis courts, and it was on a site quite near to the pavilion that two temporary class rooms were built. Ex-pupil Henrik Murden recalled that *"...they were not good places to be taught in – dreadful coke stoves in the centre of the room. They were cut off from the main school – just the place for trouble to brew. In 1944 (form) 3A were put there – a "good" form – (but) we did not live up to the school's expectations. We used to put empty toothpaste tubes on the coke stove lid ..."* Barrie heads recalled that *"... the pavilions were the evening meeting point for older boys and girls, again discouraged, but not very actively. The need, or alleged need, to re-stoke the coke boilers gave the unruly third forms a means of shortening lessons, such as the latin instruction given by Miss Weissbruth (left July 1946), whose fluency in Latin was not matched in English".* The main school was heated with coke boilers, and it was the job of school caretaker George Exley to maintain both the boilers and the pile of coke. Known as "Slacker" Exley, because of his fondness for leaning on his shovel and regaling unwary pupils with his life story, Mr. Exley became something of a school institution. One enterprising pupil discovered a more dramatic way of shortening lessons when he stopped the school clock one playtime. History does not record how he managed this feat, nor of what befell him when the authorities discovered his prank.

School routine was apt to be interrupted by startling news, and Mrs. Jean Barnstead recalled that at one school dance, Tommy Lusher appeared on the stage and in hushed tones gave news of the sinking of H.M.S. Hood, one of the country's largest battleships. When the Hotel Majestic was bombed on 12th September 1940, several Grammar School pupils saw the plane encircling the town, although they were sometimes not believed, until confirmation came through on the grapevine. Barrie Heads recalled one other occasion when lessons were in progress, and headmaster Lusher burst into the room in some consternation, just as a tremendous roaring could be heard from a low flying aircraft. Tommy ran across the room towards the window, from which a British aircraft could be seen flying towards the school from the brow of Harlow Hill. The children were entranced, but Tommy was furious, saying it was disgraceful and *"I think I got his number, He probably came from Dishforth. I shall ring up and complain!"* Some of the pupils' activities at this period included raising money for Spitfires, and Mr. Heads recalls that salvage drives were organized through the Scout and Guide groups. *"We went round with a handcart on Saturday mornings, collecting bundles of newspapers (and) occasional scrap metal."* When any old boy members of the R.A.F. visited the school, they were received as heroes.

There were several RAF bomber command airfields around Harrogate, and occasionally, a returning plane crashed, the crew baling out over town. Ex-pupil Barrie Heads recalled that boys cycled out from the school to take souvenirs from the crashed plane. On one occasion, so much was taken that the police were called, and a deeply indignant Tommy Lusher demanded that everyone handed in their spoils. Some boys turned up to school with ammunition, guns and even grenades. *"I recall boys literally festooned with belts of machine-gun ammunition. I hadn't even been to the crash site but someone had given me a single bullet. I dutifully went to Tommy's study and handed it in. "I thought better of you" he said. I was mortified to be thought one of those people who hadn't even scavenged properly".*

For the majority of pupils, the special conditions of war time did not mean an end to the routine of the school year, with its round of curriculum, examinations, and sporting events, one of which led to the accidental death of chemistry teacher Willie Wallis who was umpiring a cricket match on 20th June 1945. Bending down during the match to pick up a ball, Mr. Wallis, known familiarly as "Toto" (because of the appearance of his signature!) was struck behind the ear by a ball hit by a pupil who was batting in the nets. Ex-pupil J. Allan Patmore recalled that his body was laid in the men's staff room, and that pupils were forbidden to walk past. Mr. Wallis's death caused great shock throughout the school, and his name was perpetuated with the Wallis Memorial prize. He was replaced by Henry Hall, brother of maths teacher Jack Hall, the former being described by ex-pupil Henrik Murden as *"a completely different character whose lessons were happy times."*

The boys physical education master "Pop" Fairman, (to distinguish him from his son) who had joined the school in September 1920, was, towards the end of his career, perhaps not the most energetic of instructors, although to his lasting credit, he served as an officer in the school's Army Cadets' unit. J. Allan Patmore recalled that *"...Mr Fairman ...was much better at describing exercises than performing them. Indeed, even touching toes was a one-off, which left him beetroot-faced, and with a shower of coins rolling from his trouser pockets to the corners of the gym. We were then invited to do the same thing ten times or more. He seemed to spend much of his time sitting on a chair in the corner, keeping a benevolent eye on us whilst reading his paper to the full. He was a friendly charmer, perhaps most of all to those like me who were, to put it mildly, not of the gymnastic persuasion. In sharp contrast, girls gym was in the firm hands of Miss Duckworth, and there were no excuses tolerated there!"* Miss Duckworth, who joined the school in 1933, became one of the school's most well remembered members of staff, along with her fondness for sharp commands accompanied by short blasts from her whistle! The register of staff absences between 1924 and 1949 shows that the worst records for health were held by the two physical training teachers, Mr. Fairman, and Miss Duckworth, with the former being on sick leave repeatedly. As for Miss Duckworth, her health record was good, until July 1944, when she had a bus accident that meant she could only do a half-day's work until December 1945. It is possible that Miss Duckworth had been a victim of the black-out.

Another key member of staff at this period was Miss C.M. Andrews, the senior mistress and senior history mistress, who along with Mr. Lusher guided the school through the difficult war years; both had joined the school in 1919. Described by one ex-pupil as having "very high standards herself, and expecting the girls to live up to them", Miss Andrews was also a specialist history teacher.

Ex-pupil J. Allan Patmore has provided a clear picture of life at the Grammar School during this difficult period: *"Harrogate Grammar School in the 1940's was a unique experience, as the country went through war and the aftermath of war. The wider philosophical debates were beyond us at that stage, but we were given a thorough and enjoyable education despite all the problems which pressed in on school and society. One last memory is of a school prize-giving...when the guest speaker was General Montgomery's brother. He began, disarmingly, by noting that our expectations must not be to high – for he had not seen his brother since 1939!...But I suspect the school also recognized real heroes, for my schoolboy diary records that on 31st March 1944, "Saw Winston Churchill at Scott's corner" – way out of my usual haunts for a Friday afternoon in term time, so I suspect we had been encouraged to go and cheer. But even schoolboy heroes had their limits. I well recall when Yorkshire were playing a match on Harrogate ground not far from the school, being warned by Mr. Carr in morning assembly not to absent ourselves from school to go and see the team in action, as he would be there in person to ensure there was no truancy!"* General Montgomery's brother had been posted in 1941 to the Army Convalescent depot at Queen Ethelburga's school. Ex-pupil George Holmes recalled that Montgomery became a firm favourite at Harrogate Grammar School because of his taking groups of pupils to the Sunday evening big band concerts at the Royal Hall.

One of the periods most significant sporting achievements came with the Army Cadet Unit's football team, established largely thanks to pupil George Holmes, who was also made a Sergeant, and later, a Quartermaster Sergeant with the cadets. It may have been a sign of the school's insular nature at this time that although the Grammar School's first eleven at football, captained by George Holmes, were supported whenever they played for the school, when some of the same pupils, captained by the same George Holmes, represented the Army Cadet team at the prestigious Wetherby Lane Ground, nobody from the school turned up to support them. The Army Cadets Commanding Officer was physics teacher Major. A.R. Leathley, and ex-pupil George R. Fowler recalled that it was not unusual for Mr. Leathley to leave his pistols in an unlocked drawer, where they could be retrieved by fellow pupils. In 1944, it was clear that all kinds of changes were brewing. At the highest level, the Government's new Education Bill, sponsored by R.A. Butler, was passed, although certain clauses did not come into effect until 1947, including the raising of the school leaving age to fifteen years. The Butler Act, as it was known, divided secondary education into three kinds: "Grammar", "Technical", and "Modern", all of which were to be free, and free of means-testing, save the means of testing at eleven, which automatically guaranteed the restriction of freedom of choice to those children who failed the tests at eleven. The Butler Act was virtually silent on the curriculum, which was to be left to the area's Local Education Authority, based on local government, who were to be responsible for all education within their boundary, save that of the universities. In a move that some may have considered retrograde, the Act made the teaching of religion compulsory. Despite its weaknesses, the Butler Act was a major step forward, although it is probably true that once the Bill was passed, successive governments appear to have done their best to take back control of the curriculum, emasculate the Local Education Authorities at every step, and interfere with the art and skill of teaching whenever such a chance has arisen.

In Harrogate, changes of a kind were underway that were unlike those experienced by the Grammar School. If the demise of the nation's Spa industry was not inevitable, then it was nevertheless unclear how it would fit in to the post-war world, and talk of a national health service. An economy that relied on a small number of wealthy patients for survival would obviously be out of step with a society that expected uniform standards of treatment for all. In 1944, the Council decided to commission a report on the future of Spa treatments, published in January 1945, with rather gloomy findings. Basically, the report concluded that although some spa treatments were effective, one might obtain the same beneficial results with plain tap water. These findings led the Council to believe that a diversification of the economy would be necessary, if Harrogate was to survive economically.

The same year as the Butler Act was passed, Harrogate Grammar School pupil numbers reached 900; during a "Salute the Soldiers" week the school raised over £4,000; and the governors suspended the school's constitution of 1933, and established a temporary group of councillors to sit on the governing body, apparently because of the upheaval caused by the new Act.

It is instructive to consider the number of successful candidates for the school certificate examination during the war years. In the Autumn term of 1938, the Grammar School had 620 pupils, and an 80% pass rate, but by September 1945, 806 pupils had an 74.6% pass rate. These figures need to be interpreted in the light of wartime conditions, with a staff structure that was constantly changing, and a body of pupils that was enlarged by evacuee children who may have been partly traumatised. The highest number of entrants for the school certificate was in 1942, the year that saw the peak of the evacuations to Harrogate, and once again it is testimony to Mr. Lusher's headship that more children than ever (109) entered the school certificate examination in this year, with a pass rate of 84.5%. The School Certificate Examination required a candidate to pass in English Language (the compulsory subject) and in five other subjects chosen from at least two groups, of which groups 2 and 5 must feature.

In January 1945, Mr. Carr returned to resume his work as headmaster. During the war, he had served in the RAF, where he worked with the Rhodesian air training group and, from 1944, with the Welfare Directorate at the London Air Ministry. Mr. Carr's return meant that Mr. Lusher, who had guided the Grammar School's fortunes throughout the difficult war years, had to step aside from his role of acting headmaster, and it was typical of the man's stature that he appears to have done so without complaint or rancour. Indeed, many ex-pupils and staff have ventured the opinion that Mr. Lusher should have been appointed headmaster for life However, it was the admirable Herbert Carr who guided the Grammar School through the difficult years following the 1944 Education Act, post-war austerity, and the years of decline for Harrogate's Spa.

One of the first signs of the war's ending was the vacating of the boys' gymnasium by the A.R.P. and of the drafting of a new constitution that was set before the governors. Another sign was the announcement of an intention to publish two school magazines annually. One was to be devoted to school matters, the other to be of a literary and artistic character. The post war era was to furnish a considerable amount of material.

A.E. Thoseby, headmaster 1912-1934

H.R.C. Carr, headmaster 1934-1960

T.H. Lusher, senior master, senior mathematics master,
and (from 1940-1945) headmaster

Headmaster Ernest Gordon Carr.

Headmaster Ernest Gordon Hill.

Head Mary Dance

Head Kevin McAleese, CBE.

Head Philip Limbert

The Grammar School's first building, Haywra Crescent.
Courtesy Mr. C.B. Hopes

Girls' senior form at Haywra Crescent

A class of c.1913,
Photograph courtesy of Mr. G. R. Fowler

The stern face of education — pre-1914 staff at Harrogate Secondary School, later the Grammar School. (Back row, L to R): Mr. Wheeler; Mr. C. L. Jacot; Mrs. Rogers; Mr. Wallis; Miss Wilkins; Miss Hanna; Miss Smith (teacher of Swedish gymnastics and massage!). (Front row, L to R): Miss Hollins; Mr. Morris; Mr. Loseley; Miss Duckitt; Mr. Cowley.

THOSEBY

An early group photograph of the academic staff of Harrogate Municipal Secondary School, in Haywra Crescent. Courtesy of Mrs. Audrey Bottomley.

Girls' Senior form at Haywra Crescent

The academic staff at Haywra Crescent

Windsor Cottage, Otley Road, before the building of the Grammar School.
Courtesy Mr. M. G. Neesam.

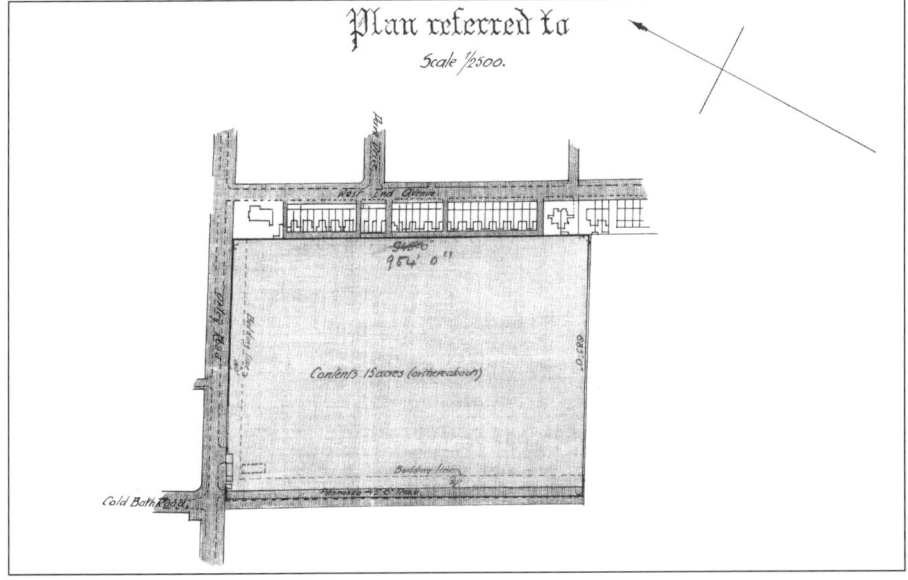

Marshall's first survey plan of the proposed new site on Otley Road, showing route
of new road, later Arthur's Avenue.

Girls' physical exercises during mid-morning break, c.1935,
with the new Arthur's Avenue in the background.

The Arthur's Avenue wing, showing the railings removed during World War Two.

The new assembly hall, c.1933

The 6th form in the library, c.1935

The 1ˢᵗ year class for woodwork

The Laboratory for advanced physics, c.1935

The Dining Hall, c.1935

The airy Gymnasium

Third year girls at work in the domestic science room, c.1935

Pupils studying for School Certificate in art, c.1935

The Library at Harrogate Grammar School

A typical class room in the new Grammar School

Mr. Kitching's form 2e

Form 1c, 1936, the notorious Ms. Jacot, form master.
Courtesy Mr. G. Holmes

The class of Mr. Thompson's remove form "B", 1938-9.
Photograph courtesy of Mrs. M. R. Barker

A junior boys form c.1938

Staff, c.1933

Female pupils, c.1933

Presentation to a retiring teacher

The female staff in the 1940's

The popular Miss Buchanan, shortly before her sudden death in 1933.
Courtesy of
Mrs. Audrey Bottomley

The imposing entrance on Arthur's Avenue

The academic staff, c.1936.
Courtesy of Mr. G. Town

Form 1.A, c.1940, with Alistair Burnett on back row, 4th from left.
Form Master Mr. S. Male. Courtesy of Mrs. Smith

A girls' form, c.1940

Mr. Jones' class at Harrogate Grammar School, c.1940

Grammar School forecourt during the Second World War, headmaster T. H. Lusher at top right. Photograph courtesy of Mr. N. Lusher

School Football Team, c. 1944.
Courtesy Mr. G. Holmes

H.G.S. Army Cadets inspection, 1942.
Courtesy of Mr. G. Holmes

The staff, c.1948

The Prefects, 1945-6

Left to right, front row: Pocock, Barrer, Wood, Heslop, Chapman, Hoare, Aufricht, Smith.
Second row: Batty, Buckle, Bolton, Ashton, Hannam, Fortune, Harris, Jackson.
Third row: Fowler, Martin, Hutchinson, Winter, Brayshaw, Flint, Penfold, Monkman, Vaughan, Farries.
Back row: Carter, Burkitt, Brown, Ashby, Walder, Hopkinson, Lancaster.

The staff in the summer of 1946, photographed by the school's photographic society.

Dedication of the War Memorial, 1948
The Bishop of Ripon, Mr. Carr, Mrs. W. Jackson

The under fifteen XI, 1948-9
Left to right, back row: R. Waddinton, J. Henderson, Mr. Fairman, C. Henderson, G. Wood, Mr Addyman, T. Wilson, A. Parker
Front row: B. Rowlatt, J. Render, M.G. Barnes, B. Barker, M. King

Miss C.H. Andrews, B.A., senior mistress,
and senior history mistress, 1919-1949

Apples for everyone, 1st May 1950 - post-war rationing meant that the gift of apples
from British Columbia was greatly appreciated.

The first XI hockey team, c.1951
Left to right, back row: Sally Horner, Shirley Taylor, Pauline Fearley, Anne Hall.
Front row: Jill Dodsworth, Clarice Hollins, Joan Collens, Mary Cundall, Joan Foster.

The First Rugby team, c.1947-8.
Photograph courtesy of Mr. G.R. Fowler

Swiss Tour group, July 1948.
Courtesy of Mrs. Monica Jenkins, (nee Clayton)

Switzerland visit, 1949.
Courtesy of Mrs. Monica Jenkins (nee Clayton)

Switzerland visit, 1949.
Courtesy of Mrs. Monica Jenkins (nee Clayton)

Sports day, c.1953

Brigadier C.W. Phillpots, D.D.O.S. Northern Command
inspects the Cadet Corps, 1954

Harrogate Grammar School Combined Cadet Force, R.A.F. Section, 1962-3

A craft department workshop, later 20th c.

In the domestic science laboratory, later 20th c.

The Grammar School team for the television broadcast,
"Youth wants to know" June 1958

Duke of Edinburgh Award Training - Mr Townend's Mountain rescue team
Grammar School and Army Apprentices, c.1958

Miss Jennings, B.A.
Deputy Head, Senior Mistress and
Senior English Mistress, 1921-1958

Miss A.C. Sharples, deputy head
mistress and senior mistress replaced
Miss Jennings after September 1959

The staff, c.1955, left to right back row: Saunders, Nixon, Walker, Mayer, Sharman, Webber, Fairman; Second row: Crother, H. Hall, J. Hall, Leathley, Foster, Carling, Jackson, Measures; Third row: Lightowler, Forrest, Elders, Millar, Black, Johnson, Harrox, Dawson, Lowcock, Parker, Morphet, Wakefield; Fourth row: Thomson, Holmes, Fisher, Duckworth, Carr, Jennings, Peters, Davison, Jones.

The Under 15 Hockey Team, c.1979
Left to right, back row: Deborah Stratton, Lisa Moore, Louise Preston, Sarah Kenny, Jane Sanders, Jane Williams.
Front row: Deborah Moon, Janine Green, Elizabeth Hooley, Ruth Clayton, Janet Peacock (Captain)

S. Downhill and P. Chilvers construct the new Cathode Ray Oscillograph
built from the kit supplied by I.C.I. Ltd

Prize Day, 1961

The 1st XI Cricket, 1961
Left to right, back row: Morgan, Iveson, Marshall, Harris, Williams, Young.
Front row: S. Smith, Leaf, Gill (Captain), Kimber, H. Smith

The cast of "Twelfth Night", December 1962

The cast of "The Linden Tree" - December 1963

Pupils making a go-cart in the 1960's

Colts Rugby XV, 1963-4
Left to right, back row: Lloyd, Lynch, Henderson, Strutt, Wall,
Middle row: Martyn, Britton, Young, Horsefield, Peacock, Midwood
Front row: Marshall, Leighton, Robinson (Captain), Allen, Taylor, Sharman

Prize Winners at Speech Day, 1967

First XV Rugby training, 1967, with Duchy Hall in the left background

Dr. Fisher with three sixth-formers outside their new block, 1969

Dr. E.J. Fisher, M.A., 1928-1970, senior master from 1951

Sixth formers meet the Prime Minister, Margaret Thatcher

Prize winner meets T.V. personalities

Guests at an evening of music arranged by the Parents' association, 24th November 1971: (left to right) Mr. G.R. Fowler, chairman; Mr. J. Thurland; the Countess of Harewood; Miss A. Johnson; Mr. E.G. Hill, headmaster.
Courtesy Mr. G.R. Fowler

Eric Saunders and pupils, with a relief map of the battle of Towton

A 1960's Prize day at the Royal Hall

Sixth formers hand over a cheque for £786 to Jimmy Saville, for the
Stoke Mandeville Hospital for spinal injuries, c.1981

"Patience", December 1982

Adventure Holidays

The languages computer facilities, 2002

The Language Laboratory in 2002

The Music Department, Autumn 2002

Chapter six

Post-war years

Herbert Reginald Colbert Carr appears to have been held in genuine affection, tempered by appropriate awe, by the majority of his pupils who in later life recalled their feelings for him. The respect felt by many for their headmaster must have been enhanced by their awareness of his stirling contribution to the war effort, as well as his abilities as a teacher. And Mr. Carr clearly saw himself as a teacher, not an administrator, although the requirements of his office necessitated his participation in both roles. One ex-pupil recalled that Mr Carr took classes through the school week as a matter of course. During his English lessons, Mr. Carr liked to set essays, which he would then discuss with each writer in front of the entire class. J. Allan Patmore recalled "*I can still hear some of the stylistic niceties he inserted into my early prose "Far too long sentences, boy. Use your full stops". For him we really tried, not only to avoid too much shame in front of the class, but because he seemed so genuinely pleased when we listened and tried.*

Mr. Carr was said to have been the despair of the authorities in Wakefield, because of his idiosyncratic way of treating administration, and ex-pupil Henrik Murden recalled that there was "*always resentment in the school over control from Wakefield...senior staff and governors felt there was an anti-Grammar School attitude in the County Council...(and) ...letters in the local papers over the period 1945-1950 showed this unhappiness...*"

In 1945, Harrogate Grammar School had 38 staff, and despite difficulties of retention, Mr. Carr managed to keep the proportion to staff to pupils at a ratio of one to twenty. Aided by such stalwarts as senior mistress Miss C.A. Andrews, senior master Tommy Lusher, and the indefatigable secretary Miss M. Harrex, Herbert Carr resumed his office, perhaps more with hope than certainty. The list of staff at this time included only fifteen names who had been at the school before the war, and of those, only Miss Andrews, Mr. Lusher, Mr. Kitching, Mr. Fairman, Miss Jennings, Mr (later Doctor) Fisher, Miss Holmes, Mr. G.E. Thompson, and Mr. E.N. Jones, had known the old school in Haywra Crescent. Immediately after the war, Mr. Kitching, the longest serving member of staff, retired. He had served the school for thirty-eight years. Mr. Elliot, the alleged conscientious objector, returned to teach metal work, and it is worth recalling that both woodwork and metal work had been curtailed during the war years because of supply difficulties. In 1946, another master, Desmond Measures, joined the school as Latin master, and instituted the playing of rugby football as an alternative to soccer as the winter game for boys. This was a significant move, and rugby came to dominate boys' games for the rest of the century. Mr. Measures [known as "Des"] appears to have been a notable character. Describing Des Measures as he was 25 years later, an ex-pupil recalled that his bark was sometimes worse than his bite. Des could shout at a recalcitrant girl *"you silly cow!"*, sometimes causing them to burst into tears, at which he would say in gentle remorse *"but why are you crying – a cow has the most beautiful eyes"* followed by a Latin quotation.

Shortly after the war, the gentle reign of Mr. Fairman, the boys' physical training master, gave way to the macho rule of Mr. Adamson, and one ex-pupil recalls how Mr. Adamson *"delighted in taking fifteen or so boys in the class, choosing the two most physically developed to help him, and then playing football against the other thirteen. He always won no matter how hard we tried"*.

It is usual for adults recalling their own school days to believe that discipline was much firmer in their time than in later times. Undoubtedly, such luminaries as Mr. Thoseby, Mr. Lusher, and Dr. Fisher had been stout upholders of the concept of self-discipline and self-control, but in a society that doctors language so as to abolish the concepts of shame, stigma, and guilt, constraint may vanish, making self-discipline a rare virtue. Accordingly, cruder forms of maintaining order may flourish for a short time, until they too are overwhelmed in the chaos that always results from total freedom to do what one pleases. At Harrogate Grammar School, discipline was maintained in the post-war period by detention, with the names of offenders read out at assembly by the headmaster. The writing of lines was also awarded, usually for minor offences, with the most severe infractions being dealt with by a visit to the headmaster, occasionally resulting in the use of the cane, or even expulsion from the school. Ex-pupil Eric H. Iveson recalled that during his years at the school from 1945-1950, the cane was used only a couple of times, and no expulsions occurred.

Ex-pupil George Holmes recalled an earlier occasion when somebody in his class placed a waste paper basket on top of the door, that fell on the diminutive Mr. Jones, who was furious when it became clear that the whole class had agreed to remain silent. Mr. Jones stormed away, returning with Mr. Carr, who threatened to thrash to entire class unless they owned up, carrying out his threat with three strokes of the cane across each boy's backside. Other boys found Mr. Carr less threatening. Ex-pupil J.Allan Patmore recalled that "the old man" was *"an outstanding head: gloriously eccentric, and with a gown way off his shoulders and acting more like a belt than a mark of academic distinction, and with a bellow of a laugh..."*

One term that recurs frequently in accounts of the male teachers of this period was that they were "gentleman", men who valued learning, self-control and thought for others, and who tried by precept and example to inculcate a respect for those attributes in their pupils. Dr. Fisher certainly came into this category. *"For British history we had*

"Chips" Fisher. He was a wonderful teacher, authoritative and humorous..." recalled one ex-pupil, another observing that *"he was always immaculately dressed –never a hair out of place".*

During the nineteen-forties, one significant aspect of life, for many people, was that of land-labour, to assist with home production of food, both during and after the Second World War. Many pupils participated in farm work during the holidays, where conditions were often harsh. Ex-pupil Henryk Murden recalled that the group of fifth formers with whom he visited a farm in the East Riding were forbidden to talk at meal times, and others remember the dour, often exploitative farmers who worked the children like slaves.

The first few years of Mr Carr's resumed headship were also those of continuing rationing. During the severest shortages, the minimum school uniform for boys was a tie (1 coupon) and cap (no coupons) whereas for girls it was a blouse (3 coupons), tunic (6 coupons) and blazer (8 coupons). By 1946, articles of school uniform could only be purchased at the school, and the school magazine announced that *"the school does not undertake the sale of second hand uniform but will endeavour to effect contacts between would-be purchasers and those who have articles for sale."* During the war period and the years of rationing, the school ran a clothing office, administered by Eric Fisher, which sold and re-sold second hand blazers, subject to the proper exchange of coupons.

School dinners were provided in the dining hall at five pence per day, which soon increased to sixpence. Ex–pupil Eric H. Iveson recalled *"they were at best moderate, but no less a person than the chairman of the governors informed us on speech day that they were, in fact, excellent. Nevertheless some disbelievers continued to spend their dinner money at Blackburn's confectioners in Otley Road. Latterly the tuckshop was re-established in school, and buns, ice-cream and pop were available in the dinner hour and morning break..."* About 400 school dinners were served, with fifteen pupils bringing their own from home. Milk was also dispensed, and ex-pupil George R. Fowler recalled that some boys used to vie with one another to see who could drink the most, the record in his day being held by one Derek Magson!

The blast walls were removed from the school's buildings during the bitter period around January 1946, Mr. Carr noting that *"our pleasure at their demolition during one of the coldest weeks of the year was tempered by the hardships we were called upon to endure".* Materials from the demolished walls were salvaged and used by a mixture of volunteers and detention pupils to remodel the north quadrangle. The ground was cleared, and lined with bricks, before being covered with a layer of gravel. An attempt to create a landscape garden in the school grounds had to be abandoned after repeated thefts, along with a plan to construct a firing range for the cadets. Mr Carr wrote optimistically of the school having a new dining hall which *"will be the largest of its kind yet provided for a secondary school...this will enable us to provide dinners for the whole school...the present kitchen can then provide an extra room for domestic science instruction. Ideally the present dining hall might become a swimming bath..."*. Mr. Carr's reference to a swimming bath expressed a long felt belief in some quarters that such an amenity was long overdue, and that the school's current use of Harrogate Corporation's municipal pool on Skipton Road was too expensive in terms of the forty minutes required for the journey to and from the school. In 1946, swimming instruction was provided to only the third year age group, and then only for one term. It was at this time that Mrs. V. Watson presented the school with a magnificent swimming cup in memory of her sons Gerald and Peter who fell in service with the RAF.

During the first year of peace, the Grammar School's range of extra-curricular activities, which had been curtailed during the war, were able to develop. Charity work, always an important aspect of extra-curricular activities, was continued and expanded. A collection of clothes was assembled for Holland, and a dozen parcels eventually despatched.

The Grammar School's orchestra continued to play an important role in the school's artistic life throughout the war years. The orchestra developed pupil's awareness of this important art within the school [as players] and outside it [as listeners] as with the school's visit to the Royal Hall, to listen to the London Philharmonic Orchestra. The director of the school orchestra at this time was Miss E.L. Groves, sister of the eminent conductor Sir Charles Groves.

A photographic society was re-created after war-time shortages, as was a Magic Society, with the encouragement of pupil George R. Fowler. The school's "house" system was reorganised, with the old colour system [red, blue, green and yellow] being abandoned in favour of a more patriotic "Tudor", "Stuart", "York" and "Windsor". The debating society, always an important aspect of life at the school, [certainly since the days of Mr. Thoseby] expanded its work. In 1946, it considered the motion that *"a woman's place is in the home"*, which was carried by twenty-three votes to four. The following year, a school railway society was established, and a marionette company was in existence. These apparently disparate matters reflect something of the mood of the post-war period.

Education [as distinct from social engineering] remained central to the Grammar School's purpose, especially since the Butler Education Act. In 1947, Mr. Carr wrote of *"the achievement of the sixth form in 1946 was outstanding in the annals of the* school. *Two open scholarships, one in arts and one in mathematics, two state scholarships; eight county major scholarships and one county music scholarship, is a result to be proud of and we heartily congratulate our successful candidates"*. Mr. Carr also wrote of the uncertain future of the School Certificate examination, expressing the hope that *"an externally organised test of general educational attainments at fifteen plus will be retained."* This was at a time when as many as 93% of candidates were passing the examination. Mr. Carr's concerns were shared by the chairman of the "Old Harrogatonian's" Mr. S. Gill, who wrote *"if the education authority carries out its plan for providing equality of secondary education for all at eleven plus, there is a real danger that our school will no longer exist as we know it"*. Mr. Gill was either unwilling or unable to explain why this was necessarily a bad or a good thing.

The winter of 1947-8 was one of the harshest since the great freeze of 1894. In Harrogate, the first snow fell on 24th January, falling continually until 30th January. On the following day, there was a snow storm, with six inches of snow. February 2nd saw a brief respite, but from the 3rd to the 8th of February, the snow fell every day, making a total of about fourteen inches. This was at a time of national power shortages, and on 13th February, the first electricity cuts occurred, plunging an already gloomy town into one of darkness. Then, on 25th February, a terrible snow storm shook the north of England, with eighteen inches of snow falling. The drifts in the rural areas were over fourteen feet in height, and icicles of record length formed around the school's two top storeys.

Pupils at Harrogate Grammar School, little over 700 of them, arrived at the school every day from a catchment that was probably wider than that of fifty years later. They arrived from the entire Harrogate urban area, including Bilton, Starbeck and New Park, as well as from such neighbouring communities as Beckwithshaw, Hampsthwaite, Pateley Bridge and Wetherby. None arrived by car, as private car ownership was still in its infancy, and petrol rationing would have made chauffeur driven delivery seem a wildly extravagant gesture. Ex-pupil J.Allan Patmore recalled the daily trek from Wetherby *"the morning train actually started at Wetherby at 8.15am, and was scheduled to take seventeen minutes. For my early years, it was invariably rostered for one of the LNER's Sentinal steam railcars – essentially a single coach carrying a small vertical steam engine as well as a passenger saloon. It was grossly underpowered for the journey up the steep grades to Harrogate, and it never arrived before 8.35am...we could walk past the prefects on duty to catch latecomers with a dismissive "train's late"...the return journey departed at 4.40pm, and had no difficulty in keeping a fourteen minute schedule to Wetherby. This gave a margin of 20-25 minutes for after school activities, before a hectic dash across the Stray; longer play rehearsals meant the later (and slower) 5pm bus..."*. Ex-pupil J. Allan Patmore calculated that during his years at the Grammar School, he walked some 2800 miles in his daily journeys, or two miles a day, for five days a week, for forty weeks of the year, for seven years.

Coming after the rigours of a war-time economy, pupils [and staff] simply steeled themselves to coping with the severe winter of 1947-8. J. Allan Patmore recalled *"strangely, the winter of 1947 leaves few memories except that the winter walk was much colder for much longer. But we were habitually dressed to keep warmth in: modern fashions would fare much worse. I suspect classroom temperatures were much below today's "comfortable" levels, but in that context schools were little different to any other places of work. Indeed, they had the advantage of central heating, which few, if any of us enjoyed in a domestic context. A vivid memory is of a much loved French master, Mr. Diggle, striding in, clasping the radiator and muttering "Ah mes rheumes, mes rheumes". In those years, our rheumatic twinges were decades ahead: he got his laugh, but not our practical sympathy."*

Something of the personal involvement of staff with their pupils welfare during this era, can be seen in two quite separate recollections from ex-pupils at each end of the decade. Ex-pupil Fred Roberts recalled: *"At the age of sixteen you were free to walk away from school and get a job; after five years at Grammar School...this is what my father expected would happen to me. He knew I was dead keen on chemistry, and he thought this meant pharmacy! He thought with a School Certificate he could get me appreticed as a dispenser in town and begin to earn some money...this was not what I had in mind....I had idly thought of becoming an industrial chemist and finishing up with the letters AIC after my name...one day...Tommy Lusher...(came)...to our house (and) presented my parents...with my examination results. "Fred has done **extremely** well, you **must** let him go into the sixth (form) where after two years he will win a County Major scholarship and then proceed on to university to study for a B. Sc. Degree in chemistry". Lusher knew he had got a battle on his hands as soon as dad expostulated that it meant five years without earning a penny, indeed it meant paying out money. But the school master had dealt with this situation before and I believe he was convinced he could win. However, I managed to chip in quickly to ask just what my results were. Lusher rapped out "He took nine subjects and passed them with five distinctions and four credits"... After Mother had served cups of tea and after another half hour or so of discussion, "Tommy" won the day and as a result it was agreed that I would enter the sixth science at the start of Autumn term in September"*

Ex-pupil J. Allan Patmore recalled the role of headmaster Carr in his own development: *"The sixth form was small, and the head as well as the subject staff took a very keen and personal interest in the next stages of our careers. Part of that guidance was recognizing the strengths and weaknesses of what the school could offer.*

I only knew the science side by repute, but on the arts side the school sought to play on its real strength in history. This was the more the case as I was perceived to have some Oxbridge potential. Surprisingly, the first faint stirrings of revolt were coming in my perceptions. Apart from Eric Fisher's inspiring classes, with a fair mix of social and economic history, I was becoming rather disillusioned with history as it now seemed to move further away from the interpretation of landscape which I loved. As one enthusiasm waned, another arose – geography...

But such a conversion was a problem for our head. Geography was still an infant university subject, and certainly not one that had advantages in the entrance stakes. So I was encouraged to persevere with history. [Mr. Carr's] tactics were clear. I took my HSC at 16, and then the following year could concentrate on Oxbridge. He suggested that I try Oxford in the December [term] for practice, and then Cambridge the following term. He knew that any scholarship winner had the right to change subjects before actually starting a course, and he was convinced we were far better prepared in history. But which college? Here he was a master tactician. I was steered away from colleges like Balliol, with several scholarships, but applications in great numbers. His wily solution was his old college, Pembroke. The examinations were concurrent for a whole group of colleges, - and in consequence for Pembroke there were two scholarships and but five candidates. I got my scholarship with these candidates, and in due course [to the disapproval of my college] changed to read geography.

Mr. Carr's interests were not all academic, as he was a skilled mountaineer, and used every opportunity to inculcate a love of the rugged outdoors in his pupils, one of whom recalled visits to Beddgelert and Snowdonia. Rock-climbing trips to Switzerland's Valais Alps, where pupils tackled climbs of over 10,000 feet and routes over ice and rock, that would probably give a heart attack to later generations of health and safety faddists, were undertaken with efficiency and skill. All this was highly unusual at the time, although eventually, such trips became the norm.

In 1947, the same J. Allan Patmore (later to become a distinguished professor of geography at the University of Hull) was one of four boys (the others being King, Murden and Noble) who went on 14th November to Manchester to participate in a history quiz on the Stuart period. The Harrogate team won by one point over Bolton's 47 points. The same year also saw the dawning of the atomic age at Harrogate Grammar School, when a party of sixty pupils visited the "Atomic Train" exhibition in York, with its explanation of the mysteries of the atom.

In these immediate post-war years, Harrogate Grammar School provided a five year course for pupils, up to the school certificate examination. "English" subjects covered

English language and literature, religious knowledge, history and geography. Languages included French, German (Dr. Mayer had joined the staff in 1946, as a former refugee from Nazi persecution in Vienna), Spanish and Latin. Mathematics included algebra, arithmetic, and geometry; science with biology, chemistry and physics. Arts and crafts lessons were available for book-binding, cookery, drawing, metalwork, music, needlework, and woodwork (taught since 1947 by the popular and respected Mr. Saunders). Finally, gymnastics and games instruction rounded off a well conceived programme of teaching. French was studied by all pupils from the first year, but only those who showed aptitude were permitted to study a second language. The shortage of science teachers (a national phenomenon) meant that science teaching for the first, second and third forms had to be curtailed.

Pupils who passed the School Certificate exam with a minimum of four credits were allowed to proceed to advanced courses in the sciences, mathematics, and arts and crafts. All advanced students in science and mathematics were expected to offer English language as a subsidiary subject.

Parents were advised at this period, through the school's introductory leaflet, that their children must not bring expensive watches or pens into the school, to ensure that such items were neither a cause of dispute, if lost or stolen, or envy, if coveted by children without such things. Parents were also told to ensure their children did not bring comics into school. Comics were seen as a pernicious plaything of the illiterate or immoral, and an enemy of reading fluency and English values. The early nineteen fifties saw widespread concern for the allegedly pernicious influence of American horror comics.

In 1948, two occurrences enshrined the school's attitude to the past and to the future. A most appropriate and deeply felt bow to the past was made on 28th September 1948 when the Bishop of Ripon, Dr. G.A. Chase, unveiled a memorial plaque to those who had perished during the Second World War. The needs of the future were also acknowledged when the Mayor of Harrogate, C. Jack Simpson (son of the great builder, David Simpson) wrote to Mr. Carr. The letter advised him that the balance of the sum that Harrogate had subscribed for her wedding present had, at Princess Elizabeth's personal request, been devoted to providing an annual prize to the head girl at Harrogate Grammar School. The first award was made to Betty Beaumont, and the Mayor commented that *"I hope this prize will always be held by the boys and girls of the school as a very special honour because of its intimate connection with the marriage of our future queen."* A corresponding prize for the head boy was soon made with the Holmes Award.

C. Jack Simpson had, with Alderman Harry Bolland and a few others, run Harrogate during the national emergency of the war, and, like his Father, had been one of Harrogate's most faithful and hard-working public servants. At the time he wrote to the headmaster, Councillor Simpson was struggling to come to terms with the report of Professor Davidson, which wrote off (somewhat cavalierly,) much of Harrogate's traditional Spa economy. Councillor Simpson was also trying to reconcile the implications of the new National health Service with the town's historic reliance on a comparatively few wealthy fee-paying patients. This was a difficult time for Harrogate.

The last significant event of the 1940's at Harrogate Grammar School, was the inspection of 4th to 7th October 1949, the first since that of 1937. After the excessive crowding of war time, pupil numbers had dropped to 725 (620 in 1937), with 327 boys (314 in 1937) and 398 girls (306 in 1939). During the 1936 term, the school had 55 pupils under the age of eleven, many of whom paid fees; in 1949, the school had two boys and four girls aged ten, and fees had been abolished, with pupils being admitted on the results of the West Riding of Yorkshire's County Council examination for primary children over eleven. One figure had remained the same as that for 1949: 45% of all children were leaving school without completing the school certificate examination. More promising news was discovered with the fact that whereas 5.84% of children had remained in the school at sixteen, by 1949 the figure had increased to 14.96%.

Post school activity was also examined by the inspectors, who found that whereas in 1935-6, an average of one boy per year had gone into the armed forces, nineteen had done so in 1947-8; this was of course the age of conscription.

The inspectors noted that the premises had not changed since the previous inspection, other than for the addition of two huts in the grounds in 1942 [nothing was said about their dreadful coke boilers!] and singled out the care-taker for the excellence of his work [can this have been "slacker"?] Recommendations included the abandonment of the library as a classroom, and the provision of rooms for music and modern languages. With the arts, the inspectors praised the school's policy of recommending that pupils selected and hung pictures in their classrooms, and suggested that a kiln be acquired for pottery making.

The final comments were reserved for the staff, opening with the observation that the headmaster, Mr. Carr, was assisted by 36 full-time members of staff, 19 men and 17 women, including one man who was an American on exchange with the senior history master (Mr. Fisher) now in the USA. With a staffing ratio of one teacher to every 23.14 pupils, the inspectors concluded that the balance was "not overgenerous". The inspectors went on, *"The headmaster still retains his love of experiment, but he is now more disposed to delegate some of his powers and to persuade rather than impose...*

his teaching timetable is too heavy, but this arises from a desire to know his pupils well and his willingness to deputise at a moment's notice in the absence of any number of the staff"

With reference to the pupils, the inspectors noted *"pupils generally enter the school in their twelfth year and on the results of an internal examination are distributed to the four forms, 1A, 1B, 1C, 1D, so that each form is of approximately equal quality. Here, they follow a common course in religious instruction, English, history, geography, French, mathematics, general science, art, music, handicraft (boys), housecraft (girls), and physical education. Grading takes place at the end of the first year. Form 2B, containing the least able pupils of the second year, continues with the same subjects, and additional English. Latin is started in forms 2a1, 2a2, 2a3. In the third year, 3c carry on from 2b, except that general science is replaced by chemistry, physics and biology..."* The inspectors discussed the wisdom of introducing a second modern language at the beginning of the third year, noting that *"...it would be wiser to postpone the introduction of German or Spanish until the fourth forms."* One sign of the post-war trend was that the inspectors noted the increased size of the sixth form, and the number of successful Higher School Certificate candidates, which had risen from four in 1936, to twenty-five in 1949.

The standard of religious instruction was praised, and the teaching of science virtually ignored, which may be more indicative of a desire by the inspectors to say something encouraging, rather than directly negative. However, the overall wording of the inspection leaves the reader with no doubt that the school still had much work to do if standards were to be raised to the school's undoubtedly high potential. The highest praise was reserved for the senior mathematics master, Mr. Lusher, who *"has served the school for thirty-five years (and) is still the most stimulating teacher of the subject, offering further opportunities to the able pupil and a wider, more general approach to the weaker"*

The report ended with a note that *"Now that war-time restrictions are being lifted, every effort is being made to return to the wearing of the correct school uniform. The good grooming of the girls reflects considerable credit on the senior mistress (Miss C.H. Andrews) and the women staff. There is evidence of training also with the boys, (whose) posture could be improved".* The inspectors noted without comment that *"the school cadet corps, army and air, are temporarily in abeyance...".* Finally, the inspectors remarked that *"the school is infected by the interest of the headmaster and his example of personal courage and adventurousness ... the school is a happy place, where both pupils and staff give much and receive much in return. That the school has increased in stature as a Grammar School is clear. There is much promise for the future."*

If much space has been provided in considering Harrogate Grammar School during the immediate post-war years, it is because this time was absolutely critical in determining the nature and direction of the school's journey through the second half of the twentieth century. Harrogate Grammar School was on the cusp of the century. Locally, more and more concerns were being expressed about the future of the Spa, and the need to diversify the town's economy. Nationally, the fledgling Health Service was part of a new mood of social awareness, which received a considerable boost with the Festival of Britain and the boom in housing construction. Change was not just in the air, but everywhere manifest, and it was obvious to governments of all colours that the key to managing this change successfully was the proper education of the nation's young people.

Chapter seven

1950's - Mr. Carr's final decade.

A housing growth rate of 26.30%, made the 1950's Harrogate's third busiest decade of expansion, as compared with a growth rate of 8.86% during the war-riven 1940's, or the 1920's record level of 29.65%. The town's population at the census of 1951 was 50,465, which rose by the end of the decade to 56,345. The expansion of the town placed more pressure on Harrogate Grammar School to cope with the local educational authority's requirements, the needs of employers (more of whom were locating to Harrogate as the Spa declined) and society at large.

A flavour of the time may be had from reading the school magazine for July 1950. Many of the Grammar School's publications over these years have such a high quality of appearance, with superb woodcuts, typography and editing, that it is tempting to see the influence of the senior art mistress, Miss M. Raisbeck, who developed a reputation as a skilled calligrapher far beyond the Grammar School's bounds. The magazine reported that a crate of apples had been sent to the school from British Columbia, which may have provided many pupils with their first taste of the traditional English fruit made scarce by the war years. A photograph shows Mr. Carr distributing the delicacies to the school, which reciprocated by sending British Columbia a supply of Harrogate Toffee. One ex-pupil recalled that a few years earlier, one enterprising boy had brought to school a decaying banana, which he allowed others to sniff for a penny a time!

The school magazine also reported that a Swiss gentleman, Monsieur le Comte Alain de Suzannet had presented the library with a twenty-five volume set of the works of Charles Dickens, beautifully bound. The library also benefited from a deposit of 500 books from the West Riding County Library, a service that came to be regarded as an essential part of school life, especially with the rise of themed topics and projects in the curriculum. According to the magazine, between 1947 and 1951, the school had won five open state scholarships, fifteen state scholarships, nine county major scholarships and nine county major exhibitions. By 1951, the sixth form seemed to be the largest of any West Riding school.

Extra-curricular activities continued to develop, with ever increasing support from the pupils. In 1950, the world famous conductor of the Hallé Orchestra, Sir John Barbirolli, allowed pupils to attend orchestral rehearsals in the Royal Hall, an experience that for many was their first hearing of a live orchestra. Until it was killed off by insensitive programming in the 1970's, the annual summer visits of the Hallé Orchestra were the peak of the town's musical life, and were central to the Grammar

School's growing awareness of the value of music appreciation.

The tradition of school prizes was by 1950 firmly re-established, the latest recipients being head boy, J.Allan Patmore, who won the Holmes prize, and Sheila Potts, who won the Princess Elizabeth prize, re-named the "Queen Elizabeth" prize in 1952. Such presentations were encouraged by the newly formed "Parents Association", which first met on Wednesday 7th May to discuss proposals with the staff. The meeting took place shortly before the retirement of one of the school's most significant characters, "Tommy" Lusher, who left at the end of the summer term of 1951. The charismatic Mr. Lusher was undoubtedly one of the Grammar School's most distinguished staff, and has been the subject of the greatest number of glowing testimonials supplied by former pupils to the author of this book. Following service in the Great War, Mr. Lusher had joined the school's staff in 1919, and served as headmaster during the difficult years of Mr. Carr's absence. An officer in the fifty-eighth squadron of the Air Cadet Corps, Mr. Lusher had a palatial mind, and gave a lifetime's service to the subject (mathematics) and school that meant so much to him. His importance to the school's academic and moral life cannot be over-estimated.

Swimming instruction was re-organised in 1951, with plans to introduce the subject at the Starbeck Baths to first year pupils. It has been a regular but fruitless activity to discuss the idea of Harrogate Grammar School having its own swimming pool. Fifty years since the ending of the Second World War, Harrogate's most important school was *still* without such an amenity: this is something that future commentators will find difficult to understand.

Outings and extra-curricular activities of a non-sporting nature continued to occur, and in 1950, included such treats as a visit to the municipal gas works, a tour of a sugar beet factory, and a lecture on the Tsetse fly by a Dr. Jackson: for some, it may have seemed that life was nothing but a round of pleasure!

In December 1951, the senior dramatic society and the senior choir combined their efforts and mounted an elaborate entertainment, which opened with a one-act play entitled "The Rehearsal" by Maurice Baring, a skit on Macbeth. The school magazine reported that *"the players grappled gamely with this difficult play, Shirley Neesam as Burbage (Macbeth) and Gillian Marsden as Mr. Hughes (Lady Macbeth) gave masterful performances, supported ably by the rest of the cast...the school choir gave excellent performances of well-known choruses from Handel's Messiah... solos were capably rendered by Sally Horner and Pat Donnelly...".* The standard of such dramatic and musical performances remained high throughout the rest of the second half of the twentieth century.

The 1950's witnessed a broadening of Harrogate's employment capacity. In 1955, ICI opened at Hornbeam, and within two years was employing 1,165 personnel. In the same year, the Post Office Savings Bank employed 1,372. Other important employers at this time included the Regional Hospital Board, Dunlopillo-Bintex, Octavius Atkinson, British Rail, Harrogate Corporation, and the West Yorkshire Road Car Company. The existence of such a variety of employment potential was certainly not lost on local schools, although as Harrogate Grammar School enhanced its reputation as a centre of academic excellence, its pupils were able to seek employment across a far wider geographic area than in the past.

The earlier part of the 1950's was economically part of the post-war economy, and although the worst privations of short supplies and rationing were over, the fat years of the Macmillan boom (*"You've never had it so good"*) lay a few years in the future. Money was not plentiful, and the concept of children earning their way through life as soon as possible, was accepted almost universally. Harrogate offered good opportunities for part-time youth employment, and in an age that had not come to terms with the later century's obsessions with regulations, employers' responsibilities and employee "rights", the majority of boys, and fewer girls, had experience of some kind of part-time employment. However, as Harrogate had always been a wealthy area, youth part-time employment was probably well below the national average. In 1951, Mr. Carr was writing in the school magazine that *"the most disturbing feature about this season has been the number of boys who prefer working (i.e. after school) to playing football, a state of affairs beyond control of the school..."*

A link from the past crept into the school magazine in 1953, with a reference to a Yorkshire Evening Post report that "Mr. Jacot, former French teacher, retired in 1943, has left England for the south of France". The magazine also noted that the George Medal had been awarded to Captain Richard Hedley Hough, a former head boy of 1941-2, who had been an Adjutant in the Bomb Disposal Unit (U.K.) of the Royal Engineers.

Ex-pupil Geoff M.B. Wilkinson recalled his experiences at Harrogate Grammar School during its golden jubilee year, 1953, which was also the year of Queen Elizabeth's Coronation: *"I had the privilege of being head boy. The headmaster at the time was Mr. H.R.C.Carr, a man of strong character and with powerful leadership qualities. He had gathered around himself some excellent teachers, and, as a science student, I was deeply indebted to the senior chemistry master of the time, one Mr. H.I. Hall, known by a number of nicknames, one of which was chemi-Hall, in order to identify him from his brother, Mr.J. Hall, who taught mathematics. It was mainly as a result of his masterful teaching that I obtained a State Scholarship and entry to Clare College, Cambridge. Whilst the school was co-ed, there was definitely a girls and a boys end of the school buildings. There was even a divide between the respective playing fields; a thick hawthorne hedge. The meeting of the sexes at breaks and in the lunch hour was strongly discouraged! Extra-curricular activities were prominent and I still have vivid memories of an Easter climbing expedition to north Wales, led by members of the Birmingham University Climbing Club. We stayed at the climbers' club hut, called "Helyg" situated near Capel Curig, and used, incidentally, by the successful 1953 Everest Team for oxygen equipment trials and general briefings. Our training was on the lesser heights of Snowdonia such as the Idwal Slabs, then on to more adventurous climbs on "Tryfan", the beginner's mountain...*

It was during my time in the sixth form that rugby arrived at the school. The set pattern of soccer in the autumn and winter, and cricket and tennis in the summer, was suddenly challenged by two incredibly enthusiastic rugby playing masters. One was the aforementioned Mr.H.I. Hall, and the other was the Latin Master, Mr. D. Measures, known affectionately by all as "Des". They introduced the game and soon got together a useful first fifteen from the non-soccer playing senior students. Both codes lived comfortably together until, to the great dismay of the soccer players, a decision was taken to confine the school's soccer features to the spring term, and to let the autumn term be used purely for rugby. What happened? - The soccer players took up the oval ball game and in no time at all, half the rugby first fifteen members had been displaced by former soccer players. In retrospect the advent of rugby added quality to the school.

A further innovation about that time was the introduction of harvest camps during the summer holidays. A small group of sixth form boys were invited to work on a large farming estate near Driffield in east Yorkshire, which at that time was owned by Lord Vesty, a very rich gentleman with many interests world-wide. The words "harvest camp" are a bit of a misnomer as we were billeted in the farmer's own house and lived the life of a farm worker. On my first visit, I was curious as to why my friends were cleaning their main course plates so thoroughly. I soon found out. The rice pudding was served on the same plate and in my case, the leftover gravy came bubbling up round the edges! After a hard day's work in the fields gathering in the harvest, bath time consisted of following each other into the same water in a large tin bath, with an extra dose of "Domestos" added in between! Two or three of us attended the local church, and in relating our story to the vicar, we were invited to the vicarage to enjoy civilised bath-times with clean hot water, large fluffy towels, and tea and custard pies to follow. Unfortunately, the farmer got to know of our new arrangements and we were threatened with immediate dismissal! We all needed the money and in most respects were enjoying the farming life so we agreed to revert to the old tin bath. I believe it was Mr. J. Hall who was responsible for organising this particular summer holiday activity.

For me, my years in the sixth form were rewarding and enjoyable, leaving me with many good memories to look back on."

The coverage given by the media to the social upheavals of the 1960's sometimes obscures the changes of the 1950's, especially regarding the growth of the teenage market, and the spread of private car ownership and foreign travel. The observant Grammar School pupil, as he or she walked through 1950's Harrogate, would have seen the gradual development of popular culture at several levels. The shops were still largely private, but the goods in those shops were targeted increasingly at the teenage market, especially fashion and music. This had a direct influence on Harrogate Grammar School, as pupils became less willing to accept the dictates of economy or their parents' or school's bizarre taste in apparel. In future, the school authorities might dictate the nature (or lack of it!) of school uniform, but if they wished to have any chance of the uniform being accepted, then attention would have to be given to style and appearance. School uniforms, in the early 1950's, were supplied by Rawcliffes of Leeds, who continued the supply throughout the century.

The enormous development of interest in music by a consumer group with an increasing means of financing that interest, led to a re-appraisal of music in the school curriculum. Although probably few contemporaries saw a connection between the cavortings of Mr. Bill Haley and the teaching of first grade viola, the link was there, if only in the phenomenal growth of the musical experience. The school also kept abreast of developments in the media, and in 1953, pupil Stella Gregory took part in a school television programme "Top Town", in which Harrogate beat opponents Hull.

In 1954, a bell, tuned to the key of E and weighing three-hundredweights, was hung in the bell tower, to commemorate the school's fiftieth anniversary. The bell was cast by Paul Taylor's bell foundry at Loughbrough, and cost £115 (collected by the governors), plus another £138 to the contractor for hanging it. The bell was no longer rung to summon pupils after the post-comprehensive additions to the school required the use of internal electric bells.

In August 1954, during the summer holidays, the Grammar School's Otley Road playing fields were leased to a commercial fair, following the previous year's visit of a fair to the Stray opposite the Prince of Wales Hotel, when torrential rain turned acres of the Stray into a quagmire. The same thing happened in 1955, when the playing fields were scarred for weeks afterwards, although the fair's promoters spent £50 on repairs. A new main drain was laid to serve the expanding housing estates to the south of the school, as yet a further example of the town's urban growth.

The retirement of Senior Art master Oliver Pemsel brought a new face to the Art

Department in September 1954, with Mr. Herbert Christie, whose knowledge and enthusiasm for the Italian Renaissance was responsible for the creation of a School Art Society. Mr. Christie's first utterance in the school magazine was his belief that *"all pupils in forms five and six should have a good knowledge of the history of British and Foreign schools of painting"*.

By the mid 1950's, the Grammar School's extra-curricular activities were booming, especially in the area of travel and foreign contacts. A visit to Bad Honnef in the Rhineland occurred in the summer of 1955, followed by a world scout jamboree at Niagra-on-lake in Canada, where the 10,000 in attendance included three from Harrogate Grammar School: J.S. Newton of the twenty-first Harrogate Group, N. Peel of the twentieth Sea Scouts, and M. Fineron, also of the twenty-first group. Mr. Carr's enthusiasm for mountaineering was behind the decision to erect an Everest Memorial to all members of the Climbing Club who took part in assaults on the world's highest mountain. Leigh Mallory was club president when he died on the mountain in 1924. The memorial, executed by Eric Saunders, added another feature of interest to the school's walls.

By 1955, the school's range of sporting clubs included a golf foundation course, with lessons provided by Mr. W. Bowman, professional at Knaresborough golf club, a revived badminton club, a basket ball club, and a new swimming club. Two years later, the school magazine for July 1957 noted the acceptance of the school by the Duke of Edinburgh's awards scheme as a source of potential entrants. This was at a time when the number of prizes awarded by the school to illustrious pupils had increased to cover such things as the Annakin essay prize, Bailey cup, chess club prize, the civil service prize, the civil service music prize, the headmaster's general paper prize, the Hitchen prize for English, the Holmes award, the Lusher prize for mathematics, the Mayor's prize for French, and the Wallace memorial prize.

The 1957 school magazine also recorded that the visitor at the 1956 prize day was Sir John Hunt, the famous mountaineer. On another page, the magazine reported that the scripture union has welcomed *"Mr. J. Neville Knox, ... Town Clerk, (who) has also been a frequent and welcome member"*. Knox's term of office coincided with the most disastrous administration in the history of Harrogate, with its deliberate closing down of the Spa, the wrecking of the townscape with crass demolitions and re-buildings, crazy traffic control schemes, plans to demolish the Royal Hall and Royal Baths, and the incompetent handling of the Conference Centre contract. He was also a religious zealot and distributed the "Good News" bible like confetti; ex-pupil Russell Davidson recalled that Knox would say *"you will burn in hell if you don't read this"*. Perhaps it was understandable that the school humoured Knox by allowing him to address the pupils, because of his influential position as Town Clerk, but from the educational aspect it was quite unforgivable. Ex-pupils recalled that Knox would rant and rave about hell fire and eternal damnation, in a vulgar and splashy manner; one ex-teacher recalled that she had secretly to arrange to have the bell rung ten minutes after Knox was due to stop, in order to quiet the man.

The school magazine for July 1957 reported several interesting matters, including the completion of the carved ceremonial throne made in 1956 by Mr. Saunders for the assembly hall's stage. This handsome piece of furniture included the names of former headmasters, and joined a table [1951] and lectern [1949], to which were added two side-chairs [1969 and 1971], and many plaques and shields. However, it was regrettable and rather mean, that the name of T. Lusher was placed at the foot of the chair, whereas those of all the other heads were placed at the top. Mr. Saunders was widely regarded as a superb craftsman who usually managed to instil a love of woodwork in his pupils, all of whom were required to make folding coat-hangers from oak during their first year. Describing a time towards the close of Mr. Saunders' career, ex-pupil Roger Bottomley recalled that when Mr. Saunders discovered that he disliked woodwork, and had no aptitude for it, he got him to write an essay describing the topics he *did* like. When Roger wrote about his favourite topics of football and cricket, Mr. Saunders was so pleased, that he gave him two weeks free lesson time. In the years to come, woodwork was dropped from the curriculum, probably due to the pressure from the academic sector, which some may have regarded as a retrograde step. The 1957 edition of the magazine also included the first reference to the new General Certificate of Education (G.C.E.) that in its ordinary and advanced levels came to play a central role in the educational life of the nation.

Harrogate Grammar School's extra-curricular life at this period was enriched through the regular meetings of the debating society, which had its origin in the training of former headmaster Thoseby, back before the First World War, and his love of dialectics. In 1956, the society considered a motion to repeal Capital punishment, which it defeated; the following year, the motion was "that this house would rather not watch television", which was carried. This was at a time when society still considered literacy an important attribute of civilisation.

Television, despite the last allusion, did affect school life. On 25th June 1958 pupils Diana Fox, Jack Spiers and Malcolm McCartney joined pupils from Queen Ethelburga's School in facing the public at Manchester Art Gallery during a broadcast of ITV's "We want to know". The occasion was made rather daunting by the fact that teams had to confront the formidable Dame Edith Sitwell, a meeting the pupils endured with flying colours.

Something of the improvement in the school's music teaching was obvious from the choice of Bach's demanding D minor piano concerto in a concert programme. The establishment of a musical and gramophone record society added to the school's musical life, with divisions for classical music and jazz. Indeed, extra-curricular activities blossomed during the affluent years of Macmillan's Government, and by summer 1958, a chess club had been formed, a science society opened for third formers and above, and so many parents were taking their children on foreign holidays that the school magazine referred to the habit in its news pages.

A gift from ICI Fibres of a kit for its new "cathode ray oscillograph", featured as the frontispiece for the July 1957 school magazine, and showed pupils S. Downhill and P. Chilvers assembling it in the science laboratory [see p.90]. The growth of extra-curricular activities at the Grammar School was supported by the governors, under the chairmanship of Alderman A.V. Milton, who gave long and distinguished service to the school. During the later 1950's, the board of governors included four Mayors, one Bishop and one Professor, and the participation of local politicians in the school's governance has been, and continues to be, a regular feature of life at the school. The governors had much to consider at this time, as the so-called post-war "bulge" generation was approaching the age for secondary education. The school asked for four further teachers to cope with the influx of "bulge" children, and built new accommodation along one side of the open corridor of the "girls end" of the school. At the same time, plans were being considered for new science laboratories, which were begun in 1959, the same year as a new deputy head mistress, Miss Sharples, was appointed, and as the publication of the government's Crowther report into the education of fifteen to eighteen year-olds.

As well as planning new facilities for the "bulge" and "post-bulge" generation, the school also smartened up some of its older facilities, and in 1959, the Parents Association effected a major improvement by removing bricks and rubble from the north quadrangle and planting grass and bulbs.

Towards the close of the 1950's, an important change occurred in the town's economy. In 1958, the King's Road rose gardens were removed to make way for Harrogate's first custom-built exhibition hall, which within a comparatively short time proved an economic success, despite ruining the appearance of the surrounding area. The reason for the Council's enthusiastic endorsement of the conference and exhibition business lay with the fear that the town's exclusive source of income, the Spa, was about to dry up, and that to ensure Harrogate's economic survival, the town must diversify. This was sound reasoning, yet the way the administration put the reasoning into effect was catastrophic. Far from learning from the previous error of concentrating on one principal source of income, the Council repeated it, by switching totally from a Spa-based economy to an exhibition/conference one. Harrogate switched from being an economy almost solely dependent on one business, to being completely dependent on another. The history of the 1960's in Harrogate town is the history of this change, a change that was reflected at Harrogate Grammar School by the extraordinary achievements of the next headmaster, Mr. E.G. Hill.

Mr. Carr, at his retirement in March 1960, could look back on a successful career. If his predecessor Mr. Thoseby had stamped his personality and standards on the old school in Haywra Crescent, Mr.Carr had done the same thing with the new school in Otley Road. When he arrived at Harrogate, the school had 630 pupils, and when he retired, it had 930. The number and warmth of individual testimonials to Mr. Carr's abilities as a headmaster and teacher, his concerns for the welfare of his pupils and staff colleagues, and his stature as a scholar, as a man, and even as a friend, all combine to reveal H.R.C. Carr to have been an outstanding figure. This opinion of Mr. Carr was shared by distinguished old boy, Professor J. Allan Patmore, who in November 1959 returned to the school to entertain the sixth form to "*a surprisingly interesting lecture on Harrogate and its historical and geographical development*". Fifty years later, Professor Patmore was to write of H.R.C.Carr that in later years he "*became a firm friend*". Very few headmasters have enjoyed such a claim to fame.

Chapter eight

The triumph of E.G. Hill, 1960 to 1980

The thirteenth post-war school magazine, issued in July 1960, advised readers that their new headmaster, Ernest Gordon Hill, had been educated at Cambridge, where he had been a Goldsmith Exhibitioner in history at St.John's College, having gained, in 1936, the distinction of being a College prize man. Mr. Hill taught for two years at Saffron Walden Grammar School, and during the Second World War, served as a commissioned officer for five years in East Africa, where he was second in command of an infantry battalion of the King's African Rifles. After the war, Mr. Hill taught at March Grammar School, Ely, from 1946 to 1948, before moving to the Joseph Lecky School at Walsall until 1954, when he then became headmaster at Waverley Grammar School in Birmingham.

The year prior to Mr. Hill's arrival in Harrogate, building work had begun on the new science laboratories, and it was science, along with mathematics and English, that came to dominate much of the curriculum of the Hill years at Harrogate Grammar School: years that were repeatedly rewarded with glittering academic success at national levels. The school magazine for July 1960 reported that the annual scholarships had included six state scholarships, nine County Major Scholarships, eight County University Exhibitions, five County Bursaries, as well as three presentations of boys at Buckingham Palace to receive Duke of Edinburgh awards. When Mr. Hill retired in 1980, Harrogate Grammar School sent 84 students on to university.

In the early 1960's, the school magazine again began to show marked improvements, both in typography and illustrative woodcuts, which were probably due to the influence of art master Herbert Christie, as well as Miss Raisbeck. Several singular references to extra-curricular activities included an invitation to the sixth form to visit Flamingo Park to see the alligator given by the school, although why Harrogate Grammar School was ever in a position to give an alligator, is a mystery. The magazine also printed an ominous account of the three minute warning in case of nuclear attack [this was the time of the Cuba missile crisis], and followed it up with a visit by four Americans from Menwith Hill to answer questions put from the floor.

Ex-pupil Colin Brittan recalled that Harrogate Grammar School's policy towards sport was partly governed by social attitudes, and that when he asked about football, he was handed the oval rugby ball and told *"football is a working class game and if you want to play it you can do so on the Stray"*. When Mr. Brittan returned in 1975 as a French teacher, rugby was still the school's pride and joy. It is an interesting aspect of changing practice that Mr. Brittan recalled that, when he was a pupil, the French teacher, Mr. Marshall, smoked during lessons, but by 1975 such behaviour was unknown.

On 14th February 1962, the distinguished local historian H.H. Walker spoke to the school on "the functions of the local press". Mr. Walker believed that it was not only the responsibility of the local press to reflect the opinions and actions of the local community, but also positively to encourage good citizenship, and discourage anti-social behaviour in all its forms. Mass circulation was obviously important to a newspaper, but not, added Mr. Walker, at any price. At this time, H.H. Walker was working on his monumental study of Harrogate under the administration of the Improvement Commissioners. It is interesting to note that Harrogate Grammar School has a long tradition of inviting historians to speak, from the 1930's, and J.R. Ogden, through to J.Allan Patmore, Bernard Jennings, and H.H. Walker in the post war era.

In 1963, Miss A.C. Sharples left her position as deputy head of the school, and was replaced by Miss Agatha Johnson, who had joined the staff in 1940. Miss Johnson was, in those days of continuing segregation, deputy head for the girls, as Mr. J. Hall was deputy for the boys. Ex-pupil Carol Arthur recalled that Miss Johnson was like *"a ship in full sail, and must have worn the most amazing undergarments"*. Miss Johnson always left a cloud of perfume behind her during progress through the school, and opinion varied as to whether the scent was Helena Rubinstein's "Apple Blossom" or Elizabeth Arden's "Blue Grass", or indeed some other brand. Miss Johnson possessed what several of her acquaintances described as a "cantilevered bosom", wore astonishing amounts of face powder, and was rumoured to have lost a fiancé during the Second World War. Ex-pupil Carol Arthur described Miss Johnson as a great teacher, who may have been formidable and scary, but who had a passion for English, and really cared about her pupils' progress. Other ex-pupils have admitted that they were terrified of "Aggie" and of her phrase *"if you fail to do so, you will be most severely punished!"*. It was Miss Johnson's whim to insist that pupils bound their exercise books in brown paper, which she then inspected for neatness. Miss Johnson was not celebrated for her sense of humour.

Although Miss Johnson is alleged to have remarked on occasion that *"a little face powder is acceptable"* she probably did not admire the uniforms worn at this time by the girls , as they were a rather ugly brown, with beige stockings ribbed like corrugated iron. Later, American tan was worn, and some girls rebelled by wearing Marks & Spencer clothing. The introduction of tights had a huge impact as they allowed girls to wear much shorter skirts in the era of the mini-skirt. Ex-pupils recalled that some boys were always dropping pencils in the immediate vicinity of short skirts. Most girls developed the habit of rolling their waist bands up, to make their skirts shorter, so Miss

Johnson started checking skirt length with a measure!

Staff wore gowns at this time, although by the later years of Mr. Hill's administration, only about half of them continued to do so. The gowns provided an air of dignity and authority to the staff, and it has always been customary for all pupils to stand when a teacher enters a classroom.

Madame Wolf, who taught French, was another notable personality. Ex-pupil Carol Arthur recalled that Madame Wolf gave the impression of goose-stepping along school corridors, wearing knee-length boots. She was not a figure to mess with, and was very right-wing in her views. Carol Arthur recalled that Madame Wolf had once made her remove a Liberal election poster from the car she drove as a sixth-former, but was not above hanging National Front posters in the sixth form room. Madame Wolf eventually dropped her support for the National Front as the party became more extreme.

The school magazine for July 1963 reported the death of an ex-member of staff, Monsieur Jacot, who died in France at the age of eighty-three, having been French master for thirty-eight years. By the time of his death, Monsieur Jacot had acquired mythical status in the school's folklore, and ex-pupils were now talking of Jacot having thrown one tiresome boy through an open window, and of dangling another over the stairwell of the old Haywra Crescent building, and threatening to drop him! The same school magazine also paid increasing attention to academic success, with 55 pupils gaining GCE's. The school population had now risen to over 950, and the sixth form to 150, and Mr. Hill warned the school that seventeen to eighteen year olds were threatened with an excess of exams, due to increased competition for university places.

April 1963 saw a start being made on two new laboratories for "A" level work in physics and chemistry, and the division of the library into two classrooms. The old dining room was converted into a substitute library, and the kitchen into a small classroom. Something of the spirit of the school at this period may be found in the decision to form a combined cadet force. Recalling his experience of the cadet force in the following decade, ex-pupil Russell Davidson has described the school's rifle range and armoury, located at the end of the playing field, which enabled cadets to fire .22 rifles. The thick blue woollen RAF uniforms in which cadets drilled were worn at school, and became very hot in quite short a time. The cadets were also able to attend RAF camps at Church Fenton and other places, where they had the opportunity not only to fly, but often to pilot trainer aircraft.

By the close of 1963, the school had forty-nine teachers, and nearly one thousand pupils. One ex-pupil from the years 1957-1965, Professor Russell Betts, recalled

"...*some of the excellent teachers during my time. Many had served in World War 11, and had gone to their studies later in life than usual and therefore had a more mature attitude. Of particular note were the Hall brothers, Jack (maths) and Henry (chemistry). Both (were) fearsome characters who stood for no nonsense and for excellence. They, together with Mr. Sharman (physics) and Miss Bessie Black (maths) formed my early scientific thoughts and gave me a superb grounding which I continually fall back on*" Other ex-pupils, perhaps less academically gifted, have recalled the Hall brothers less favourably, claiming that their manner could be intimidating.

The mid 1960's were critical years for Harrogate. Since 1947, the state had been sending national health service patients to Harrogate for spa treatments in the Royal Baths. However, in 1964, Leeds Regional Hospital Board announced that from April 1968, no more national health patients would be sent to Harrogate, a decision that was potentially fatal for Harrogate's nearly 400 year old Spa industry. The council took private advice, which reported that there was still sufficient private business to keep the Spa alive, provided that the service remained first class, and the council persevered. In the event, the council kept the Royal baths open for a mere twelve months, before closing it altogether. Within a further year, the same council disconnected the pump at England's oldest Spa, the Tewit Well, which had been in continuous public use for exactly four hundred years, turned off the supply of Magnesia Water in Valley Gardens, broke up the unique well heads in Bogs Field, and placed advertisements in the Financial Times for the redevelopment of the Royal Baths. The wrecking of the spa not only created fresh urgency to develop the conference and exhibition business [as it was intended to do] but also opened the way for the further diversification of the local economy, and the resulting urbanization of the townscape. Although the 1920's were Harrogate's busiest single decade for development, with a growth rate of 29.65%, the town's cumulative growth rate between 1951 and 1981 was a staggering 67.46%, which placed enormous pressure on schools and other services.

In 1964, the school magazine reported a discussion at the school between Town Clerk Knox and journalist and historian H.H. Walker, in which the former argued that the town must move *with* the times, and the latter warned that the town must not be moved *by* the times unless the times were the right times. The same magazine contained its first reference to a new popular musical phenomenon called the Beatles, and a warning from Malcolm Proctor of the folly of proposed plans to demolish Sir Giles Gilbert Scott's magnificent Foreign Office in Whitehall, to make way for another concrete and glass monstrosity of the kind that was already being foisted on the public at Harrogate Railway Station.

Labour Governments from 1964-1979 [apart from the short-lived Conservative Government of 1970-4], promulgated the ideals of comprehensive education. In conservative Harrogate, the introduction of the comprehensive system was not welcomed. The trend towards comprehensive education had at first been opposed by the Labour Party, who then became converts, and supported plans to phase out grammar schools in the name of social justice. This was social engineering on the grand scale. In 1965, the newly elected Labour Government instructed all local education authorities to prepare plans for the creation of comprehensive schools, either by amalgamation of existing sites, or by new building. In consequence of policies followed both by Conservative and Labour Governments after 1965, the majority of grammar schools had, by 1990 become comprehensives or independent..

The educational policies of the time may have come as a shock to Mr. Hill, who had been appointed before the comprehensive debate reached Harrogate. It is clear that from the start of his headship, Mr. Hill was determined to improve and enlarge the Grammar School's sixth form, as well as increase the school's overall academic progress. Something of Mr. Hill's heroic efforts to expand the sixth form can be seen in the fact that by 1965, 225 of the school's 1,000 pupils were in the sixth form, and that due to an increasing school intake, the first year had five forms. When the 1967 magazine was published, Mr. Hill was able to add that the sixth form had increased to 230 pupils, and that the school's exam results were still comparing favourably with the national average; 169 pupils had, within the year, sat successful GCE "0" level examinations, "A" level results were excellent, and fifty-five pupils had gained entrance to universities. During the period between 1968-9, the sixth form increased to 320 pupils.

Each year, pupils were divided into six streams, ranged by intellectual ability: at the top came A.1, then in descending order A.2, A.3, B.1, B.2, and finally "R", assumed by some to mean either "retarded" or "remedial". In judging this system from the standards of another age, it does at the very least appear to have been divisive and a guarantee of massive resentment by those who were not classed as A.1. Whether or not such resentment was a good thing [in that it encouraged the less able to work harder to attain higher status] or a bad thing [in that it was unfairly elitist and ensured the best resources were lavished on a minority of pupils] is a matter of opinion. It is significant that the sources of the most glowing commendations for the school during this period have all come from academic high-fliers, whereas opinions that the school failed to encourage their potential came from ex-pupils who had been given lower gradings, many of whom went on to achieve great success in later life.

One story may add to readers' understanding of Mr. Hill's attitude to the streaming at this period. One ex-pupil recalled that after he had been very cheeky to his teacher, he was sent to Mr. Hill for the cane, whereupon Mr. Hill asked him if he was in the A.1 stream, and intending to sit for Oxbridge. On hearing confirmation of his suspicion, Mr. Hill merely told the cheeky pupil to go away and behave! The implication of this response was that a less able pupil would not have been treated so leniently. Now this was precisely the kind of selective administration of a penalty that infuriated opponents of corporal punishment in schools, and which led to its abolition by a society that was becoming increasingly obsessed with equality.

Harold Wilson's "White heat of Technology" theme coincided with the appearance in 1968 of the Dainton report, which examined the flow of candidates in science and technology, into higher education. This had been partly predicted in Mr Hill's 1967 speech day announcement that *"in the near future, science students would find little difficulty in gaining places [in universities] but arts, social sciences and business studies students would face a shortage of places"*. The same year saw the first use of computers in the school, which proved "particularly popular".

In 1966, the West Riding County Council settled the future of secondary education in Harrogate, in conformity with Circular 10/65 that all education authorities should make a choice as to which style of *comprehensive* school organisation should be adopted in their particular areas. In some respects, Mr. Hill was fortunate, in that his headship did not require the assimilation of so many Government reports, compared, for example, with his successor, the unfortunate Mrs. Dance, who suffered from an excess of them. Between 1960 and his retirement in 1981, Mr. Hill had to face the implications of the Crowther report of 1959 [education from 15 – 18], the Newsome report of 1963 ["half our future"], the Robbins report of 1963 [higher education], the Dainton report of 1968, the James report [teacher education and training] of 1972, and the Waddell report of 1978 [school examinations]. Other reports, such as the Vernon report of 1972 into the education of the visually handicapped, or the Rampton report of 1981 into West Indian children in schools, probably fell outside Mr. Hill's immediate sphere of concern. His successor, Mrs. Dance, had within her ten years at the Grammar School, from 1981 to 1991, to contend with eleven Government reports, and a corresponding amount of legislation, increasing standards and measurements, and all the other devices that enable bureaucrats to meddle in the teaching profession.

July 1968 saw the retirement of Mr. G. E. Thompson, Head of the languages department, who had been with the staff since 1931, and who later had responsibility for teaching German. At this time, the school retained only one member of staff who had known the old school in Haywra Crescent: Dr. Fisher, whose brilliant submission on the Yorkshire estates of the Percy's had gained him a Ph.D. In some respects, Dr.Fisher had gained the respect once accorded to Tommy Lusher, save that T.L. coming from on older generation, had been seen by some of the younger female staff as a rather intimidating figure, whereas Dr.Fisher seems to have been regarded by his younger colleagues as a more approachable individual. For many pupils however, Dr. Eric Fisher, who taught Latin and history, *was* formidable. Some ex-pupils recalled that Dr. Fisher would not allow any crossings out in homework, so groups of pupils gathered before his lessons and used dissolving ink to remove errors. At his last school speech day, in 1969, Dr. Fisher, who had been with the school since 1928, admitted to having *"rather pessimistic views of comprehensive education. Mistrustful of great and sudden change, he would regret deeply the loss of individuality of the Grammar School, and suggested that we in England are about to copy what the Americans are now abandoning"* Dr. Fisher, known affectionately as "Chips" Fisher, had succeeded Tommy Lusher as Second Master. One ex-pupil recalled that at his retirement, Dr. Fisher stood up and said *"well, it really is goodbye Mr. Chips"*.

Dr. Fisher's 1969 reference to comprehensive education was telling. As far back as 1957 the school magazine had referred, jokingly, to "the Otley Road comprehensive", but until successive governments began meddling in local education, the idea of Harrogate Grammar School becoming comprehensive remained a joke. The theme was taken up by the Chairman of the Governors, Alderman A.V. Milton, who took the opportunity offered by the centenary of the Forster Act of 1870 to warn parents that education had by 1970 become subject to excessive bureaucratic control. The Parents' Association, now under the chairmanship of George R. Fowler, was alerted to the threat, and began to arm itself for the struggle over the issue of comprehensive education.

This was the time of the Vietnam War, and some pupils at the Grammar School demonstrated their feelings by painting the words "Yanks out" across the roof of the school. A prank that seems to have entered the school's folk memory was at one morning assembly, when just as Mr. Hill was mounting the platform, a recording of Benny Hill's vulgar song "Ernie the Fastest Milkman in the West" rang out from behind the stage curtain. Mr. Hill was said to have been furious, and the whole school called to a special assembly and given a severe warning, a reaction that some may have considered was a humourless response to a silly prank. The offenders, said to have been threatened with expulsion, were never caught. Another memorable prank was the hoisting of Mr. Hill's favourite chair from the school roof.

Extra-curricular activities continued to thrive under Mr. Hill's headship, as they had done under his predecessor, Mr. Carr. During the 1968 to 1969 school year, the Grammar School's rugby team had achieved outstandingly good results, which were acknowledged widely in the press. *"Never in the history of Harrogate Grammar School has the first team produced such an outstanding set of results"*. After ten successive victories, the full colours were awarded to all team members. Some outstanding victories included Hipper-holme (14-3), Bingley (12-0), Castleford (10-0) and Morley (19-0). At the same time, the combined cadet force was re-organised, with the Army section being abandoned and the RAF section enthusiastically organised by the kindly Mr. Stearne, an ex-AF officer, who taught chemistry.

In July 1969, a visit to the school by 47 students from Werl, in Germany, once again emphasized the schools' strong German connections, which dated back to the time of Dr. Mayer and others. The Germans' visit coincided with the opening of the new sixth form block, which Mr. Hill probably viewed with unalloyed satisfaction, in view of his unceasing efforts to build up the sixth form. In the school magazine for July 1970, Mr. Hill reported that 169 pupils had obtained GCE "0" levels, and 135 "A" levels; 75 pupils had gone to University, with nine going to Oxford or Cambridge, and four obtained open awards. These were indeed excellent academic results, but even better were to come

In 1970, Mr. J. Hall replaced Dr. Fisher as senior master, and Mr. H. Hall, senior science master of 25 years, announced his plan to retire. He had joined the school in 1945 and became senior science master in 1955. The previous year Miss Harrex, who had been appointed secretary to the head in January 1946, became bursar, a tricky post to hold at a time that was clearly going to be one of transition. One link with the past that was severed in 1971 was with V.C. holder Archie C.T. White, who died on 20th May. Archie White had attended the old Haywra Crescent School, and had been a friend to both A.A. Thomson, and the school's other V.C. winner, Donald S. Bell. Back in 1935, author A.A. Thomson had immortalised both of his school friends in his wonderful novel "The Exquisite Burden" which told the story of a Harrogate boyhood in the distant days before the Great War. A.A. Thomson, who had also taught at the Grammar School, himself died on 22nd June 1967, at the age of seventy-four, the proud possessor of an MBE.

Ex-pupil Roger Bottomley recalled that at this time, one of the school's outstanding masters was Daniel [known as "Danny"] Glover, the senior modern languages master, who had re-joined the staff in July 1944. Ex-pupil Ruth Coombes recalled Mr. Glover's lively lessons in the 1930's. Mr. Glover possessed a wonderful dry wit, that always made him [Roger Bottomley] laugh, even when directed towards himself. Another ex-pupil, Carol Arthur, recalled Dan Glover as "*a great man*" who reeked of tobacco, and wore his gown at a rakish angle. Several ex-pupils have reported that Mr. Glover had a good sense of humour, despite rumours that his nerves had been damaged during war-time service with the Desert Rats, an experience that may have been the cause of his constant smoking between lessons, as well as his shaking hand. Ex-pupil Russell Davidson recalled that if a pupil did a really good piece of French translation, Glover would bellow "*are you trying to put me out of a job?*"

The Parents' Association chairman, George R. Fowler, was quoted in the school magazine of July 1971 as saying that parents were very much concerned with the review of secondary education by the Claro Education Executive. This concern had brought about a meeting in December 1970, at which over 400 parents had expressed their support "overwhelmingly" for secondary education being continued on selective lines, and control over post-16 education remaining with the school. Despite this example of local democracy (or more probably, because of it) the Claro Executive recommended to the West Riding County Council that secondary education should be re-organised on comprehensive lines in Harrogate. On 15th April 1971, the Claro Division's Education Officer of the West Riding County Council, Mr. J.V. Rawcliffe, wrote to the chairman of the working party of the Harrogate Schools' Association, Mr. P.S. Allen, that the Claro Division's adopted recommendation for the reorganisation of secondary education in Harrogate foresaw (1) the amalgamation of Harrogate High School and Granby Park School; (2) Harrogate Grammar School to be brought up to building regulations standards and extended to provide an eight form entry further education school; and (3) Harrogate number three school (built on field number 4953 off Rossett) to be extended, and to develop its own sixth form. Let it be noted that the reorganisation was carried out without any reference to either professional bodies or to parents.

Public concern about the proposed educational changes could be seen in the Harrogate Advertiser's correspondence columns for 8th May 1971, with letters from the Chairman of the Grammar School Parents' Association, outlining the disquiet. The Parents' Association, under the Chairmanship of George R. Fowler, tried to prevent the introduction of the comprehensive system in 1973, making a sound case for delaying until 1975. All 67 staff members signed a letter of objection to the 1973 adoption date, and a clearly worded case explained that the adoption of 1973 would ensure that comprehensive education was introduced to the Grammar School two years before the building improvements had been completed. The fears of the Grammar School Parents' Association were shared in large measure by Mr. Hill, who on 6th March 1972 wrote to George R. Fowler with suggestions for a letter to the Department of Education and Science. The letter's two principal points were (1) that comprehensive education should not be introduced until the Grammar School had all the necessary buildings and facilities; and (2) that parents and staff were disquieted because there was no open discussion about methods of allocating children to the new schools..

In the editorial to the school magazine for July 1972, the editor wrote of "...*the winds of change [which] though they have not yet reached gale force, have certainly begun to blow more strongly. Perhaps the most startling news was the size of the grant to be made available for enlarging and extending the present buildings to enable the school to meet its new educational role in Harrogate, though doubts about the readiness of our buildings to meet imminent change have not yet been entirely allayed..."* It may or may not have been the "winds of change" that caused the Library ceiling beneath the science laboratory to collapse during the school year of 1971-2, but development was certainly in the air. To the astonishment of the chairman of the governors, Alderman Milton, it was estimated that £500,000 would have to be spent on the school before it could take on its new comprehensive role. The magazine also reported that during the previous year, Harrogate Grammar School's exam results were 188 pupils with "O" levels and 137 with "A" levels. 74 of these pupils were to go on to University, 35 to polytechnics and 17 to Colleges. Mr. Hill added that *"All these academic successes...depended on the right sort of pupils coming to the school at an early age".* By "the right sort", Mr. Hill can only have meant the sort selected for academic success.

In September 1972, the Claro Divisional Executive of the West Riding sent a letter to all parents setting out details of the catchment area for Harrogate's five comprehensive secondary schools: Harrogate Grammar; the amalgamated Harrogate High School and Granby Park; Rossett High School, St Aidan's School and St. John Fisher. Along with the Borough of Harrogate, the catchment area covered the parishes of Felliscliffe, Follifoot, Hampsthwaite, Haverah Park, Killinghall, Pannal, Ripley, South Stainley-with-Cayton, Birstwith, Bishop Thornton, Clint and Menwith-with-Darley, Harewood, Kirkby Overblow, North Rigton, Weeton, Blubberhouses, Fewston, Great Timble, Little Timble and Norwood. Admission to the five schools was by parental preference, but where this distorted the allocation programme, determining factors were to be (1) those who lived and attended school outside the borough (which immediately disadvantaged Harrogate's own children), (2) those who already had brothers or sisters at the school, (3) those who had verifiable social or medical claims, and finally (4) those who lived nearest to the school. These considerations, with some variation in special cases, were what the parents received in the autumn of 1972.

Harrogate Grammar School was fortunate at this time (1969-1974) in having the services of ex-pupil George R. Fowler as an energetic chairman of the parents' association. He wrote many letters to the relevant authorities (including several to M.P. James Ramsden) making known the reservations felt by many to the changes being forced by central government. On occasion, Mr. Fowler found himself in the position of saying things that needed to be said by Mr. Hill, which could not properly be voiced by the head himself. Mr. Fowler has also recalled that when the education authority offered Mr. Hill the headship of a sixth form college, separate from the Grammar School, Mr. Hill turned it down "emphatically", saying he already had a very good sixth form at Harrogate Grammar School.

Mr. Hill's headmastership from April 1960 until December 1980 opened at a time of unalloyed support by the governors, as well as society, for a selective system of education. Yet when the same Mr. Hill retired, the governors were legally obliged to support the comprehensive system, which the government believed it wanted. Whether the reader agrees or disagrees with the premise that the comprehensive system is a dilution or strengthening of the educational process, many believe that it is the best means of ensuring that a broadly humanitarian education is within the reach of the greatest number of tomorrow's citizens. And there are many who have always believed that the "renaissance man", with a broad appreciation of the arts, humanities and sciences, is a better developed human being than one crippled by a narrow specialism. It is testimony to Mr. Hill and to the school's excellent set of staff, that throughout the length and breadth of his headmastership, not only did academic standards continue to rise, but the needs of the new comprehensive intake were also met. It was also thanks to Mr. Hill that the Grammar School retained its prestigious name.

Ernest Gordon Hill has sometimes been portrayed, at least to the author of this book, as a man obsessed with success in higher education, or, to put it crudely, with university fodder. Such an estimate would be both inaccurate and unfair, as Harrogate Grammar School continued to improve its extra-curricular and sporting activities, at the same time as it maintained its superb academic results. During the 1971 school year, the rugby first XV won fourteen of the nineteen matches it played, guest speakers included H.H. Walker, who talked about citizenship and the community; a new film society, the Wellington Club, was established, and the number of field trips increased, including continental visits of the kind first introduced by Mr. Carr.

The July 1973 edition of the school magazine sounded the key-note of a fateful year: *"from next September, parental choice* (this was incorrect, as the proper term was "preference"!), *rather than recognised ability will be the operative factor in determining which pupils enter the school at eleven plus, though the change to a fully comprehensive school will not be complete for seven years."* Mr. Hill gave what some listeners may have heard as a valedictory address at the last speech day of the pre-comprehensive era, quoted in the school magazine: *"the headmaster discussed the role of education in general. Its purpose, he stated, lay somewhere between the fostering of individual excellence and social engineering. In the past, able children received more than their fair share of attention. He did not suggest that we should go back to that system of preferential treatment, but firmly believed that while we must do our best for all children, the able child should not be forgotten in our concern for the slow learners, or remedial children... Mr. Hill spoke in defence of the external examination as a test of national validity, without which, standards would be more likely to fall than rise".* Mr. Hill also had the gratification of announcing that the 1972 external examinations had produced one 185 pupils with "0" levels, 144 pupils with "A" levels, and seven with open awards for Mathematics, Science and History at the universities of Oxford,

Cambridge and London. In his closing remarks, Mr. Hill spoke in the defence of grammar schools, which he considered had been the prop and pivot of our national system of education.

The school magazine that reported so fully on Mr. Hill's speech day remarks, also contained a photograph of the school play "The Importance of Being Earnest" that some brave souls had selected for production. Mr. Hill's response to this artistic choice of title is not known, but it is worth recording that the inspirational teachers Alan Boddy and Shirley Wells were responsible for turning around the school's dramatic productions. The production of "A Midsummer Night's Dream", in modern dress, was another remarkably successful effort, and, as ex- pupil Carol Arthur recalled, caused Mr. Hill to tell her she was *"the Jayne Mansfield of Harrogate Grammar School"* !

Other announcements in the 1973 school magazine included the retirement of the senior art master Mr. J.A.H.S. Christie, whose 1954 appointment made him a long-serving teacher. Many affectionate stories are told of Mr. Christie, his toupee, and his singular mannerisms. Ex-pupil Carol Arthur recalled Mr. Christie in the 1960's and his dealings with special classes of girls; he was given to issuing aesthetic advice and remarked, *"Now girls, always stick with white china and you won't go wrong".* Mr. Christie's great love was the Italian renaissance, and it was rumoured that his home contained casts of Michaelangelo's "David". Ex-pupil Russell Davidson recalled that Mr. Christie was the devoted son of an Edwardian mother, and that he had said he had kept all her clothes and feather fans. Mr. Christie was also given to wittering on if anything displeased him. He retained a supply of jam jars as water containers for his art classes, and if one broke, he would moan endlessly about it. On one occasion, the pupils pre-arranged a breakage and then startled Mr. Christie by each producing two replacement jars for their art master, in a great heap, piling them high on his desk, a just as he began to witter. The author recalled seeing Mr. Christie's singular progress along central Harrogate's James Street, which he negotiated with a pronounced mince, hands clasped before him, as if contemplating some question of aesthetics! Some pupils have recalled Mr. Christie's manner of stroking the hair of favourite male students. Mr. Christie's replacement, Ian Dowlen, must have had his work cut out in covering those aspects of the curriculum that Mr. Christie had ignored such as German expressionism, cubism, etc. Another master to retire at this time had even longer service than Mr. Christie, as the senior English master, Mr. S. Nixon, had been appointed in September 1945. None of the teachers at the school now had any recollection of the old building in Haywra Crescent.

In 1970, Harrogate Grammar School was still a fully selective institution (a policy supported by the governors and parents) as were Harrogate's other secondary schools, such as Wheatlands: the difference being that eleven-plus successes attended the

Grammar School, whereas its failures went to Wheatlands. Ex-pupil Carol Arthur recalled that the socially divisive nature of this arrangement sometimes produced fights, occasionally involving local skin heads and squaddies too.

Harrogate Grammar School became comprehensive in 1973, one year after the Local Government Act that brought about the reorganisation of local authorities: a foolish and morally suspect action that at a stroke cost Harrogate both its council and Mayoralty. From April 1st 1974, Harrogate town, without reference to its citizens, found itself no longer a West Riding borough, but rather now shackled to an economic cripple known as "North Yorkshire", thus ending a thousand years of history. It was from this time that really began the process of intense meddling, by both county and national bodies, in local affairs that were [and still are] entirely within the ability of local people to administer

July 1974 saw the school magazine reporting on progress with a group of "temporary" buildings in the school yard, which had been designed to cope with the increased comprehensive intakes. These lasted many more years than originally intended. The rebuilding was taken as an opportunity by the more progressive teachers to end segregated staff rooms, a move that was strongly resisted in certain quarters. Eventually, the staff rooms were desegregated, although new divisions were introduced with staff rooms for smokers and non-smokers !

Mr. Hill's next speech day included the announcement that the teaching staff had risen to 71, with 1,250 pupils and a sixth form that numbered nearly 300. Within two years the figure increased to over 1,400 pupils, including a sixth form of over 300, and examination successes that same year numbered an impressive 185 pupils with "O" level and 135 with "A" level passes, of whom 78 were to go on to university, including 9 admissions to Oxford or Cambridge. Not withstanding these successes, many thought that the school had become too big.

Changes to the teaching staff at this time included the death of Mr. A.R. Leathley, science teacher since 1946, and head of middle and upper school. Mr. Leathley's death left only four teachers from the pre-1950's: Mr. J. Hall (1936) deputy head, Miss A. Johnson (1940) deputy head, Mrs. B. Farres (1940) mathematics, and Mr. D. Glover (re-joined July 1944), the senior modern languages master. Such staff, together with their colleagues, helped create the outstanding school over which Mr E.G. Hill presided so efficiently. This is not to say that Mr. Hill was without his critics. Some former pupils have spoken of being propelled against their wishes into lines of study for which they had no affinity, and others, acknowledging their academic success in certain fields, nevertheless considered that other skills had been suppressed.

Ex-pupil and parent Peter Barnwell recalled a visit he and his wife made to meet Mr. Hill and be shown over the school, before the admission of his son, who later took successful degrees in physics and music. After being shown round the school by Mr. Hill, including visits to the English and science departments, the Barnwells pointed across to another block, and asked what function it served *"Oh that. I believe that's the art block, and all that nonsense"*, Mr. Hill is said to have retorted airily. Another parent, after a tour of inspection, was invited by Mr. Hill to attend the school's Gilbert and Sullivan recital, but was cautioned to *"have a stiff gin and tonic first"*

Some ex-pupils have reported that Mr. Hill adopted an autocratic approach to examinations, courses of study, and even university applications or choices of career. One pupil recalled Mr Hill's horror when the academically bright boy told his headmaster that he wanted to study domestic science, as he intended to become a chef. After a long struggle, Mr. Hill gave in (a rare event), and the pupil was allowed to follow his chosen subject and went on to become a successful cook. Ex-pupil Carol Arthur was made aware that as a girl at the school from 1967-1974, she was not expected to aim too high, despite her "A" stream status. Teaching was regarded as an appropriate career, "lesser" posts being considered suitable for the "B" stream. When Carol Arthur voiced her wish to become a journalist, Mr. Hill tried to dissuade her from this career choice, and she recalled that many "B" stream pupils were "written off", yet in later life became very successful, despite, rather than because of Mr. Hill's highly selective system.

If some ex-pupils have voiced resentment at the manner with which they believe they were coerced into following a particular line of study, others have spoken more favourably of the system. Professor Russell Betts has written that during his time at the school (1957-1965) the academic standards were rising, and that thanks to Mr. Hill's pushing, Oxford and Cambridge were then taking pupils from state schools. The Professor recalled asking Mr. Hill about the difference between Oxford and Cambridge, receiving the reply *"at Oxford you wash the bath before you get into it!"*

Kenneth Lowe, the head of mathematics, recalls the battles he and other teachers had to persuade Mr Hill that a mixed staff room was appropriate, now that the school was fully co-educational. Mr. Lowe also recalls his struggle to get Mr. Hill to accept that early entry for GCE "O" level was a good idea, and that for the most able pupils, Cambridge was at least as acceptable as Oxford! The legislative changes of Mr. Hill's time were absorbed successfully, commented Mr. Lowe, largely because they were ignored, whereas in later times the changes were so many and ill-thought through, that there was little hope of successful absorption. Mr. Lowe emphasised that despite the common perception that Mr. Hill cared only for his Oxbridge results, this was not true. *"Yes, he did value them, but his school and his staff did an excellent job for many thousands of pupils"* This observation has been submitted by a great many others, such as a former head of history, who wrote that following the introduction of comprehensive education, *"academic standards were maintained, and most of the less able children also did well"*

Reports of Mr. Hill's fastidious pursuit of high academic excellence, together with an apparent disdain for the arts, gives a very inaccurate picture, and one which Mr Hill seems on occasion to have fostered himself. However, Mrs. Anne Nicholson recalls that when she and her husband owned and ran Harrogate's celebrated music shop in Parliament Street, Mr. Hill was a regular customer, and was privately very interested in widening his musical horizons. This was certainly not the action of a man for whom the arts held no attraction.

Miss J.M. Clark, of the English department, and head of the library, who began working at the Grammar School in 1957 and retired in 1992, recorded her opinion that the changes of the 1970's and 1980's were generally handled well, although there were initial problems in dealing with less able pupils. For most of her time at the school, Miss Clark felt that the school compared favourably with other schools known to her, and that it held high standards of both academic excellence and discipline.

Judging from personal recollections, the use of corporal punishment at Harrogate Grammar School appears to have increased during the years of Mr. Hill's headmastership, although this assertion may be due to the greatly increased number of pupils, rather than a deliberate policy. Some ex-pupils recalled that they were lined up outside the deputy head's office, and then called in and told to lean over an armchair, so that the headmaster could apply the punishment, before dismissing the offenders. Corporal punishment was abolished in state schools by 1987, which simply reflected the fact that society no longer had the stomach to direct such severity against offenders. Within a very short time, the abolishers would turn their attention to language, and send strong words into the wilderness already occupied by strong deeds, thanks to the increasing power of the "politically correct".

One sign of Harrogate Grammar School's increasing participation in charitable work was the raising of over £1,200 towards the building of a children's ward at Cookridge Hospital, a wholly admirable deed that again focussed the attention of the public on the school's public activities. The 1977 school magazine provided a full report, as it did for the completion of the new block for music, the new sports hall and gymnasium. The same year saw the retirement of Miss Johnson, the senior mistress, and deputy head, who had joined the school in 1940, and the magazine reported the death of Mr. Kitching, at the age of 95, who appears to have been the school's first woodwork master. Another passing was announced in 1978, with the death of Dr. Fisher, who had been with the school from 1928 to 1970.

Following the 1974 arrival at the school of Adrian M. Mosley, staff cooperated in arranging "adventure holidays", which were intended to give young people a taste for outdoor life. Especially memorable holidays included those in Wales, in Normandy (with much sailing) and in the Ardeche (for the canoeing) in the south of France. Mr. Hill supported the staff in these activities, although as staff member Colin Brittan recalled, the holidays were taken in the staff's own time.

The 1977 school magazine closed with comments from the chairman of the governors, Councillor F. Rotherham, that Mr. Hill was *a lion among educationalists*. The facts had spoken for themselves, as the current year's figures showed that 215 pupils had obtained "0" levels, and in mathematics, an amazing 48% of pupils obtained grades "A", against the national average of 10.7%.113 pupils passed two or more "A" levels, of whom 72 went on to university. The school's previous chairman of the governors, Alderman A.V. Milton, had died on 7th February 1977, after long and dedicated service to the school, but the Milton connection with the board of governors remained with his son, Councillor J.V. Milton, continuing the family service.

One very important extra-curricular activity at this time was the work of a group of sixth formers, who became engaged with voluntary workers in starting a talking newspaper for people with visual disabilities. The "Talking Newspaper for the Blind" went from strength to strength, and eventually became established as a full time venture, with a studio at Ripley Castle, and a sophisticated method of distribution. Harrogate Round Table arranged a "top score" darts competition, and over £2,000 was raised for a tape recorder. At this time, the producer was L.C. Maule, the secretary Joanne Marks, and the chief editor, Elizabeth Colebourne.

The Conservative government's 1980 Education Act, called by some the first attempt to create a market in schooling [thereby betraying their ignorance of centuries of rivalry in private education] gave parents a greater say in the activities of maintained schools. Henceforth, parents of pupils were to be allowed to elect one or two members of the governing body. The other significant effect of the 1980 Act was the creation of a single school examination for sixteen year olds with grades from one to seven. It was claimed that in the preceding few years, Harrogate Grammar School had sent more pupils to Oxford and Cambridge than Eton.

During the 1980 prize day, Mr. Hill reminded his audience that seven years had passed since the eleven-plus examination had been replaced by parental preference for their childrens' school. Prizes were distributed by the headmaster of Queen Ethelburga's school, Mr. Kingdon, who advised the assembly that Harrogate Grammar School was *"a school which ... definitely and unashamedly aims for excellence".* Queen Ethelburga's, along with Ashville College and Harrogate Ladies College, was one of Harrogate's most prestigious schools, but under E.G. Hill, Harrogate Grammar School was simply the best state school in the country, so far as academic results were concerned. The following year, Mr. Hill was able to announce that the school had 1,600 pupils, with a sixth form of 300, "0" and "A" levels well above the national average, and 84 pupils going on to university. Nor had the school's charitable work suffered from the academic brilliance, in that the sixth form were still working on the Talking Newspaper, and moneys were still being raised for a whole swathe of charities. The school magazine for July 1981 showed sixth formers presenting T.V. personality Jimmy Saville with a cheque for charitable application.

By 1980, E.G. Hill had been at the Grammar School for 21 years, and the time had come for his retirement. It was later said by Mr. Hill's professional colleagues that he did not welcome retirement. Indeed, for a man so clearly committed to the school, such retirement may have been unwelcome. Teacher Wendy Cross recalls being in the staff room at the time of the interviews for the head's successor. Mr. Hill burst into the staff room in some apparent heat, exclaiming in a loud voice *"it's a woman".* However, the parting of the way had, inevitably, arrived, and amidst all the congratulations, expressions of thanks, and goodwill for the future, there was a feeling that an era had ended, and that the new and fully comprehensive system was going to come into its own, with all that that implied.

Summing up the Hill years is not easy, but nevertheless necessary. The author has received such a variety of contradictory reports about the headmastership of E.G. Hill as to make *any* judgement suspect. When E.G. Hill was appointed in 1960, the selective system was in full flow, and generally supported, at least in Harrogate. When Mr. Hill retired, Harrogate Grammar School was functioning as a comprehensive school, and moreover, one that was still achieving excellent academic results. This was no mean achievement. By any account, E.G. Hill was a brilliant producer of university material. Yet more must be said. Whereas recollections of Mr. Hill's predecessors and successors have produced comments of a warm and affectionate nature, the author has not received similar comments about E.G. Hill. At the very least, this shows that for the admittedly tiny number of ex-pupils with whom the author spoke, Mr. Hill was, and remained, a distant figure. Some ex-pupils have gone further, and spoken of their lasting resentment at feeling marginalized by Mr. Hill's alleged pursuit of high academic excellence, their numbers being too high to ignore.

Chapter nine

Enter Mary Dance, 1981 to 1991

The newly appointed headteacher, Miss G.M. Marston (soon to become Mrs. Dance) took up her position in January 1981, at the opening years of the new Conservative government, and a time of unprecedented meddling by politicians in the educational life of the nation. Anxieties were growing about Harrogate Grammar School's ability to cope with the economic requirements of change. Mrs. Dance soon touched on a sensitive issue when she warned that schools were being required to consider their curriculum [in the light of national criteria put forward by the Department of Education] at a time of intense economic retrenchment. There were also the implications of the 1978 Warnock report into special educational needs, which envisaged *"that some children with certain kinds of handicap should have their special educational needs provided in an ordinary school"*. This last matter was highly contentious, in that some educationalists feared that provision for the special needs of some children would be diluted if they had to be applied in the context of the average classroom, whereas others feared that some pupils would be held back by the slower pace required for the successful application of special needs lessons.

In 1987, Eileen Boag was appointed assistant teacher for modern languages, and, for "special needs". Before this time, pupils in the special needs category (i.e. with below average ability in English and mathematics) were termed "remedials". From her viewpoint of 2003, Eileen Boag recalled that in the early days of her service at the Grammar School, all the pupils were taught "civics" and attended school speech days when the Mayor was present. By 2003 however, "civics" had been superseded by "personal and social education", that appears to have been introduced during the 1990's, following Mrs. Dance's retirement.

One sign of change was the holding of school speech day in October, rather than April, partly because the achievements of the previous year were fresh in the mind at the start of a new term.. This was hardly revolutionary, and typified Mrs. Dance's initial caution at Harrogate Grammar School, in that changes were to be thought through, rather than introduced for change's sake. Mary Dance had previous experience of comprehensive education, as she came from St. John's School in Marlborough, which had been a Grammar School merged with a comprehensive school. One of her earliest impressions of the Harrogate school was that it had a good atmosphere with friendly, polite children, and a superb staff. She also took pleasure in the school's appearance, as *"the building exuded solidity and good design"*. There was still talk about a swimming pool, but no more than talk. Another matter recalled by Mrs. Dance was the attitude of the Parents Association, members of which could be *"demanding...[but]...in a nice way"*. During the earlier part of her headship, Mrs. Dance was able to continue to teach (religious education or history), and considered that it was important to ensure that all first year pupils came into contact with the head of their school. For a brief time, Mrs. Dance also taught a few of the sixth form. In her capacity as a teacher, Mrs. Dance was maintaining a tradition that is known to have reached back at least to Mr. Thoseby, as well as Mr. Carr and Mr. Hill. However, the ever-increasing burden of administration meant that Mrs. Dance was unable to find the time to teach, a situation that also had to be faced from the start by her successor, Kevin McAleese.

The head of the school's history department for the period between 1962 and 1986 recalled that the good relations between the teaching staff and the head teacher, so apparent (if occasionally stormy!) in Mr. Hill's time, continued to be excellent under Mrs. Dance. This same member of staff also recalled that the school's system of pastoral care tended to be minimal, which reflected other observations made of the 1940's by George Holmes, or by Colin Brittan of the 1960's. Guidance on life in the post-school world certainly seems to have been started by Mr. Hill, but it was Mrs. Dance who appears to have nurtured it until the service was of real use to all the pupils.

In July 1984, the school magazine reported that the examination system was (again) under review. After November 1984, entry to Oxford and Cambridge universities by exams taken in the seventh term of the sixth form was to be discontinued, and replaced by exams taken in the fourth term. Other universities used "A" level results to regulate their admissions. Despite cuts made in the number of available places, 140 pupils had gone on to degree courses from the upper sixth form. The continuing success of "0" level mathematics was shown by the fact that 48 out of 49 entrants had made the "A" grade.

Mrs. Dance touched on the alarming increase of government communications at this time, and noted her regret that *"education had become a party-political matter"* and that there was *"an increase in the number of outsiders telling schools what to do"*. Between 1983 ("Teaching Quality") and 1991 (DES Circular no.12/91), no fewer than seven landmark papers appeared on the subject of teacher appraisal alone.

The 1985 school magazine carried notice of two retirements: Mrs. P. Stuffins (English), who had joined the staff in 1967, and Mr. Sharman (Physics), who had joined in 1952. Several ex-pupils have recalled the visits organised by the former teacher to theatres at Harrogate, Leeds, York, or Stratford, as part of the English literature curriculum, or simply for the appreciation of drama or the organising of school plays. Drama of a different kind had occurred at the school in the summer of 1984, when it was used in the film "Wetherby", starring Vanessa Redgrave.

In several respects, the mid-1980's were key years for education, in that the 1985 Department of Education and Science paper, "Better Schools" represented a high point in an attempt to achieve a national curriculum within a tri-partite partnership of central government, local educational authorities, and schools.

The 1986 Education (no.2) Act affected profoundly the control of schools and what was taught in them. It brought together issues of parental choice, parental involvement in schools, and clarified the purpose of teaching. Places on the governing body were distributed almost equally between the local education authority, parents, teachers and the local community. The knotty issue of the school curriculum was to be agreed by the LEA, governors and the head teacher, and parents were to be kept informed. Special authority was given to the governors over the matter of sex education, in that they could decide whether to give any or none.

One aspect of the changes in society, as reflected in the legislation for state education, was the abolition of corporal punishment in state schools. Henceforth, the dramatic rise on a national level of indiscipline in classrooms, the decline of self-control, assaults on teachers, vandalism and other criminal activity, could be charted by social historians brave enough to face the jeers of the politically correct who expected others to cope with the situation they created. Harrogate Grammar School, however, was fortunate in that unlike the majority of less favoured schools, it had usually been controlled by individuals possessing sufficient authority of character to maintain order by whatever means were at their disposal.

The 1987 re-election of the Conservative government with its manifesto of introducing a school curriculum *"which will develop the potential of all pupils and equip them for the responsibilities of citizenship in tomorrow's world" and "pupils should be entitled to the same opportunities wherever they go to school"* was a pointer. The curriculum was defined almost entirely in terms of academic subjects: mathematics, English and science, with a leavening of technology, art, music, geography, history, and physical education as a sop to the secondary school teachers who were generally opposed to a national curriculum

The meddlers could not, however, leave well alone. In 1988, the "Education Reform Act" appeared, after long and bitter debates in the Commons and Lords. After a ringing opening statement about the general purpose of education, echoing the famous 1944 Act, the first part of the Act placed the curriculum within the broad context of the needs of society and pupils: *"the curriculum should be balanced and broadly based, and should (a) promote the spiritual, moral, cultural, mental and physical development of pupils at the school and of society, and (b) prepare such pupils for the opportunities, responsibilities and experiences of adult life"*. In other words, the object was to do what good teachers had long been doing!

Sections 106-111 of the 1988 Act gave governors unprecedented power to levy charges for activities connected with the school. Although admission charges were not to be made, nor charges for any in-school curricular tuition, a wide range of school activities came within the realm of fee-paying. In brief, the intention of the 1988 Act was to hold the school, through the governing body, accountable to parents to a greater extent than before. The 1992 Act further reinforced the Act of 1988.

Mary Dance had been at Harrogate Grammar School for barely one year when the face of Harrogate was changed by the addition of a new, and very important building: the Conference Centre. Whatever the public thought of the Conference Centre's design, the building set the seal on Harrogate's transformation into a successful conference town. The cost of this transformation poisoned relations with the rest of the Harrogate district, and the ratepayers of the town. For almost twenty years, the district was seldom without voices of ratepayers raising the spectre of the Conference Centre's rising costs, which eventually reached £34 millions. The 1980's saw a rise of the service sector in Harrogate, thanks to the ever-increasing numbers of visitors to exhibitions or conferences. Consequently, Harrogate came to possess more cafes, pubs, restaurants and wine-bars than ever. Use of these facilities may not always have been anti-social, but the concentration of entertainment venues in the town at a time when standards of behaviour were becoming looser, inevitably had a ripple effect.

During the 1980's, drug consumption became a national problem, and Mrs. Dance recalled that although she was aware of the nature of this problem, it did not have any appreciable impact on life at Harrogate Grammar School. In another area, Mrs. Dance acknowledged the changing attitude towards school uniform, in full recognition of the fact that uniforms were a safe issue against which young people could rebel. In order to prepare school leavers for the world in which they would soon be expected to live, especially universities where no dress code existed, school uniform for sixth formers was abolished. This was a move calculated to offend the traditionalists, but whatever the public thought of it, it was nevertheless an experiment that perhaps had to be made.

Another issue of contemporary relevance was the introduction of computers to the school, which occurred towards the end of Mrs. Dance's ten years as head. Intended at first as a tool for the Grammar School's administration, computers, inevitably, became a tool and subject for instruction of the pupils.

Mrs.Dance encouraged the school's role in extra-curricular and charitable activities, which flourished during her administration. On 9th December 1988, the Harrogate Advertiser reported that the school had raised £5,468 for Killingbeck Hospital, and the following year, the same paper for 10th March reported that at its third "annual grand sale", £600 was raised, and that Octavius Atkinson had given £1,000 towards the new computer and physics department. The disappearance of the school magazine at this time, probably because nobody wished to have the responsibility for its continuation, meant that much of the school's history can be traced only through private recollection, or examination of the contemporary newspapers.

Not all of the amenity improvements at this time were for the pupils, in that provision was also made for staff participation, such as the five-a-side football matches, the bridge club and the club for badminton, all started by energetic teacher Colin Brittan, himself an ex-pupil of the school.

At the start of 1989, the Harrogate Advertiser reported that recent falls in the number of secondary school children in Harrogate were coming to an end. For almost ten years, the number of children in Harrogate town's five state schools had gone down, and the system of parental preference meant that some schools suffered more than others. During the final years of Mr. Hill's administration, pupil numbers reached an all-time high, but thereafter began to fall. For example, at Granby High, which at its peak housed more than 2,000 pupils, the figure had dropped by 1989 to 1,015. Harrogate Grammar School, with 1,540 pupils, was again the largest school in the town.

During the 1980's, Harrogate town experienced the beginnings of a revolt against the increasing rate of housing development. Although the town's increase in housing for the 1980's was only 8.86% (compared with the 1960's 20.40%), it was an increase that came on top of the phenomenal increases of earlier decades, and for such organisations as the Harrogate Society and its successor, the Harrogate Civic Society, it was an increase too far. In future, Harrogate Grammar School would have to come to terms with the fact that it could not reckon on a permanently expanding urban population to justify a corresponding expansion of its own infrastructure. The politicians would have to apply the brakes.

The local newspapers carried Grammar School news that reflected the times. For example, in 1989, the school received the following publicity: on 16th March, the Yorkshire Evening Post reported that Harrogate Grammar School was the first in Yorkshire to adopt "healthier eating", as part of the North Yorkshire education authority's new look school meals service. The interest of parents, as well as pupils, in post-school life was shown by the Harrogate Advertiser's publication of a sixteen page supplement "Street Talk", containing information and advice for school leavers on topics such as handling money, job applications, etc. The Grammar School's regular commitment to working in the community was demonstrated by the creation of a mural to hang in County Hall. In September, the Yorkshire Evening Press reported that Harrogate Grammar School was embarking on a half-million pound scheme to build a new sixth form block, and upgrade computer facilities. At this time, the school was also attempting to improve its facilities for transport connected with extra-curricular activities, and the following year, Harrogate Motors sponsored a £14,000 minibus for field trips and sporting events.

As Harrogate Grammar School had no significant proportion of pupils from Britain's racial minorities, the school did not have to divert its resources to addressing any related issues, and as Mrs. Dance observed, *"to make such matters an issue would be like talking in a vacuum"*. However, the whole topic of inter-faith relationships, with its ethnic overtones, was examined as part of the Religious Education curriculum.

One of the biggest issues facing the school during Mrs. Dance's term as head teacher was that of the local management of schools, which came as a considerable challenge to the staff, who were used to such things as budgetary issues being resolved by the local education authority. Consequently, it was necessary for the school to obtain the services of a professional bursar, leading to the appointment of ex-banker Dean Whitehouse.

Towards the end of her term as head teacher, Mrs. Dance had to face one of the consequences of Harrogate Grammar School's being tied to the apron strings of the impoverished North Yorkshire Education authority. A somewhat sensationalist article in the Yorkshire Evening Press for 29th November 1990 informed readers that the 1600 pupil Harrogate Grammar School was about to close, because *"it had never been filthier"*. Problems had (all too predictably) arisen after the power to appoint cleaners had been taken away from head teachers and given to the bureaucrats at County Hall. The cleaning difficulty was eventually resolved, but in hindsight, the problem appears to have been fanned by claims from opposing politicians, which caused the most tremendous uproar at the time. Unfortunately, the problem of poor cleaning recurred, and still has not been resolved at the time of writing.

As information technology expanded towards the end of the 1980's, Mrs. Dance became aware that the school was going to need a computer-literate hand at the tiller, an awareness that was in part responsible for her decision to retire in December 1991, after eleven years' service. One of the last photographs of Mrs. Dance to appear in the press before her retirement was on the 26th November 1991, when after two years' work to raise money, work began on extensions to the school. One of the fund raising activities included a direct appeal to ex-pupils. The £210,000 extension scheme to provide six extra class-rooms and a new sixth form block, got underway when Mrs Dance cut the first sod, and told reporters *"This new building represents a testament* to the partnership between the school and the local authority. When they saw how much money the parents were raising, they felt more inclined to hand over the rest." Since the appeal was launched by TV personality John Craven, £90,000 has been raised by parents, staff and pupils, a truly heroic success.

Mary Dance has admitted that her time at the school missed the worst of the problems resulting from the change to comprehensive education, but that many of the system's initiatives still had to be managed. Relations between the school and the county were excellent, as they were between herself and the staff. In summing up her time at Harrogate Grammar School (which most objective viewers would judge to have been difficult years from the point of the post-comprehensive change, and the rate of outside intervention) Mary Dance has identified three of the school's best attributes: (1) a superb staff, (2) children who were friendly and able, and (3) parents who were supportive and ready to rally round when needed.

In one of her final press statements, Mrs. Dance gave vent to her irritation with government policies. The Yorkshire Evening Post for 13th November 1991 reported the Grammar School's head teacher as saying *"I have I suppose what is an impossible dream...that education should cease to be a pawn in the party-political game and become instead the beneficiary of some kind of concensus whereby all parties agreed on adequate funding and then gave schools a long period of stability before making any further changes"*. Mrs. Dance went on to attack the Government's Assisted Places scheme: *"It diverts money which might otherwise go to ensuring that maintained schools are adequately funded. For the same reason I regret the advent of City Technology Colleges; these represent another way of helping the few instead of the many."* Attacking school league tables, Mrs. Dance went on to give the shrewd judgement that although she was pleased Harrogate Grammar School featured well up in two national newspaper tables, *"I think only those who know a school and the area from which the pupils are drawn can make any attempt to assess its success, while in-depth judgment requires a knowledge of individuals."*

One of the most lasting of Mrs. Dance's legacies was the introduction in 1991 of a school newsletter, "The Link", which built on the parent-teacher newsletter, and presented news of Grammar School life. It is still going strong at the time of writing.

Chapter ten

Century's end - the McAleese years

It is fair to say that Kevin McAleese's term of office at Harrogate Grammar School was one that witnessed acceleration of government interference in education, a growing awareness of the role of management, the domination of computers, the pervasive influence of a media that had become increasingly crude as the decade progressed, and an increasing tendency to litigate (or threaten litigation) to resolve complaints about pupil treatment.

On seeking a replacement for Mary Dance, the governors of Harrogate Grammar School had to ensure that any new head was a strong character: one capable of implementing the changes required by the Education Acts of 1988 and the pending 1992 Act. The former Act necessitated the appointment of a head who could manage the school's own budget, now the equivalent of a sizeable business. One of the reasons for the appointment of Kevin McAleese was that he had been head of a secondary school in Essex that had been a pilot for the introduction of the new LMS system. He also understood the role of computers in education, and grasped the fact that this role could only be an increasing one.

Mr. McAleese was appointed head teacher from January 1992, and when the new Education Act appeared, it seemed as if Local Education Authorities would remain the essential engine of both local and national educational systems. Yet moves were afoot within the new Conservative government to reduce the power of LEAs to the residual status proposed by the 1992 White paper "*Choice and Diversity*". As in the 1980's, government policy of the 1990's led to the inescapable conclusion that the Conservatives had a detestation of the Local Education Authority. It was in this atmosphere that the 44 year old Kevin McAleese took up his post.

Born in London, Kevin McAleese had travelled the world as an officer in the Merchant Navy, before deciding to go back into higher education at the age of 21. The school into which he moved in 1992 had 1,610 pupils and 101 teachers. One of those teachers, Mr. G. Brian Newton, had joined the staff back in 1965 as head of German and had been head of the sixth form and deputy head since 1972. Mr. Newton held his posts until his retirement in 1992, by which time he had made significant contributions to the school's academic progress, particularly in modern languages, as well as assuming overall responsibility for the new levels of financial independence given to schools under the 1988 Education Act. The new extension to the sixth form block, opened in 1992, was named the Newton wing to commemorate Mr. Newton's contribution to school life.

By October 1992, Mr. McAleese, after consulting parents, authorised changes to the girls' school uniform, which now adopted the boys' colour of black; a change introduced partly because of the declining quality of brown cloth. *"I feel that smartness is very important, to the image of the school, and hope to make the wearing of blazers compulsory in the near future"* explained Mr. McAleese to the press. The following month, teachers were giving their reactions to the first national publication of school exam results, some of which were described as *"grotesquely misleading."* Although Mr. McAleese's comments were less harsh than those of other local heads, probably because the figures showed that Harrogate Grammar School was doing well, he warned parents to treat the government's figures with caution. The Spring of 1993 saw the introduction of tests for fourteen year old pupils. Then in May, after massive disruption and controversy, the standard assessment tests were abandoned after a national boycott by teachers' associations.

Less troublesome publicity arrived in October 1993 in the pages of the "Independent" newspaper, which reported that Harrogate Grammar School had won eight places for students to Cambridge University, which was more than many selective or fee paying schools. In commenting, Mr. McAleese's words revealed something of the revolution that had occurred over the previous thirty years, saying that the school trained its pupils in public speaking and gave them mock interviews which helped them succeed in the tough entry procedure. *"We are not saying Oxbridge is the best place to be, but we are saying that if our students think they would benefit then they should try"* the head was quoted as saying.

Head teacher McAleese's next public utterance was aired in the press with the following set of controversial school league tables to be published, assembled with data that contained rather too much simplification for most educated opinion. Writing on behalf of the Harrogate and District Secondary Head Teachers Association, Chairman Kevin McAleese and Secretary Dennis Richards (head of St. Aidan's school) wrote at the end of a long and constructive letter that *"parents in the Harrogate area have nothing to fear about standards in their schools and should rather fear being misled by the data published today"*. This eloquent response was published just above a statement from the headmaster of Ashville College, who shared the current disquiet with the Department of Education's figures. By November 1993, Dr. Hallas, chairman of the governors of Harrogate Grammar School, had the gumption to write to Education Secretary John Patten, to tell him to "stop meddling". He was only interested in payment by results and in overloading and dictating the curriculum down to the finest detail, said Dr. Hallas, who also accused Patten of imposing *"tests, tests and more tests"* and of squeezing out elements such as music and arts which had little value in the market place but were vital to the development of the whole person. Had they heard them, her words would probably have been applauded by earlier heads such as Thoseby and Carr.

September 1993 saw the establishment of a school "senate", with the purpose of giving pupils the opportunity to be involved with the running of the school. Ideas put into practice included giving sixth formers lockers with keys, and the obtaining of a £1,000 grant towards establishing wildlife (unspecified!) in the quadrangle. At this time, Harrogate Grammar School was also raising £7,514 for the relief of Rumanian orphanages, as yet a further example of exemplary charitable work.

A principal problem faced by Harrogate Grammar School in the 1990's was one of structural decay. Despite extensions and "patch and mend" repairs, the 1933 building was showing signs that it needed a considerable amount spending on repairs and modernisation. In rectifying this unsatisfactory state of affairs, the head and governors were restricted by provisions of the 1988 Act, which had given schools the theoretical advantage of controlling their own budgets [as distinct from being controlled by the Local Education Authority], but which thereby placed a huge additional administrative load on the school's head. One of the many consequences of this change was to ensure that Mr. McAleese, unlike all his predecessors, was prevented from doing any teaching other than occasionally standing in for absent colleagues, or taking school assembly. The neglect of the Grammar School's own clock, which had been vandalised in 1981, was made good in August 1993, when Mr. Abholt restored the 1932 Potts clock. For many years, a story circulated in the Grammar School that the clock and its tower had been built as an alternative to a swimming pool, an unlikely story given the difference in constructional costs, and one the author has not been able to verify.

In 1995, Mr. McAleese faced the alarming news that a corridor outside the school's dining hall had collapsed; fortunately, without causing any injuries. Steel beams had then to be fixed in all the main corridors, and the ceilings had to be lowered. This was only three years after a £25,000 refurbishment of the school library, that was funded by the Parent-Teacher Association. 1995 was also the year the Education Minister, Gillian Shephard, visited the school.

During the 1980's and 1990's, when the Grammar School's structural problems became apparent, Harrogate town suffered from the legacy of the Conference Centre's costs, especially in a reluctance to spend anything on maintaining public buildings. The increasingly ruinous state of the Sun Pavilion, Market, Royal Hall, and Royal Baths' Western Wing, were eloquent witnesses to this legacy. Indeed, the demolition of both the Market building and of the Royal Baths Western Wing [both built in the same decade as the Grammar School] showed that the Grammar School was not the only building in the town to suffer from what some called "concrete cancer", but which others termed "neglect".

Mr. McAleese's awareness of the structural problems faced by Harrogate Grammar School, and the likelihood of the heavy financial expenditure required for improvements, was partly the cause of his support for the school's bid to opt out of Local Education Authority control and to become fully grant-maintained by the government. This was to be a contentious and divisive issue, although some of those opposed to the "opting out" option must have been aware of the difficulties faced by the school arising from the 1988 and 1992 Acts. The action favoured by Mr. McAleese did not receive sufficient parental or staff support, and was rejected at a key vote. Teachers Wendy Cross and Eileen Boag recalled that the "opting-out", or "grant maintained" issue produced extremely strong feelings on both sides, but that staff did their best to ensure that the tensions produced were kept away from pupils.

The "opting-out" issue created tensions with some of the school's governors, although the chairman of the time sided with Mr. McAleese. However, many of the other governors opposed the head. One of the governors, Liberal Democrat Councillor George Crowther OBE, who later became chairman, was vehemently opposed to the proposal to take Harrogate Grammar School out of the control of the Local Education Authority, and even went so far as to call for the head's resignation on local radio. To say the difference of opinion between the head and some of the governors over the "opting out" issue soured relations, would be an understatement. The relationship between the head and certain governors was thereafter an uneasy one.

One effect of the 1988 Education Act was that Harrogate Grammar School lost its ability to decide what was taught, following the adoption of the National Curriculum. Mr. McAleese believed that as there would always be a demand in Harrogate for a sixth form that could provide for admission to universities, the post-1988 ethos for competition in league tables made inevitable the school's concentrating on academic success. Also, he felt there appeared to be little opportunity in Harrogate for school leavers of sixteen years of age.

The involvement of parents with school activities was largely a post-war development. Although such involvement was widely and understandably welcomed, it nevertheless had an aspect that some may have considered unwelcome: the politicisation of education. Although this was nothing new, the pace of such politicisation increased, and from the 1980's onwards, press reports of educational disputes tended to reduce them to the ideologies of opposing political parties A local example may be found in the dispute over the "right" of parents living in villages around Harrogate to send their children to the school of their choice in Harrogate town, which thanks to the league tables, ensured that Harrogate Grammar School was very often the school of their choice. In itself, this "right" was harmless, but when parents with similar views, who lived in Harrogate town itself, also tried to exercise the "right", they found that village children had precedence. The trouble with rights is that when everyone has equal rights, nobody has any rights, as this squabble showed.

The "right" to take drugs was something that really hit society in the 1990's. Mr. McAleese told the Harrogate Advertiser that *"One thing must be made clear. Like the fear of crime, the fear of drugs was worse than the actual problem"* Yet this was not a matter of the head sweeping an inconvenient problem under the carpet, as Mr. McAleese went on to admit that he knew drugs were *"out there"*, and that *"some of his pupils... will come into contact with them outside the school"*.

Mr. McAleese recalled that excellent relations were developed with the police's drug squad, and that the drug situation was closely monitored, so that it was rare for any pupil to try to bring drugs into the school. Mr. McAleese also recalled that during his time as head, only two pupils were given permanent exclusion orders (in other words, expelled) for drug-related offences. Following a meeting, to start an important campaign against drugs, chaired by the Harrogate Advertiser's Editor-in-chief, Jean MacQuarrie, a statement appeared in the newspaper that *"Under-age drinking and the crime related to it is a bigger problem"*.

The drugs issue was a feature of the school's participation in the Observer's "Mace" debating competition, patronised by Lord Hailsham. Harrogate Grammar School won through to the finals at the London Oratory on 6th May 1994, pitted against Brentwood School, who were opposing the motion that "this house would legalise the use of cannabis". Harrogate's team included Kieren Hollingsworth and Katy Maclean, who won the debate in favour of legalisation, an outstanding achievement. Winning the debate was a highlight of the decade, and when the Mace was brought to Harrogate, it was proudly displayed in a glass case until it had to be returned to the Observer the following year.

Smoking by pupils has always been banned in the school, but because it was legal for sixteen year olds to smoke, something had to be done to control their smoking. Sixth formers were told not to smoke within the school's immediate environs, and if they were caught breaking this rule, were made to pick up cigarette butts in Arthur's Avenue, Otley Road and West End Avenue. Ex-pupil Carol Arthur recalled that in the late 1960's and early 1970's, before publicans' identity cards were introduced, underage drinking was easier than in later times. Mrs. Arthur identified Otley Road's "Salt Box", Crimple's "Traveller's Rest", and Harlow Carr's "Harrogate Arms" as being popular with sixth formers.

The Grammar School faced other social problems. Kevin McAleese, throughout the 1990's, was aware of the potential problem of the paedophile menace, and of the security questions facing the school. A telephone warning system was introduced, whereby the police contacted the school if known offenders were in the locality. The influence of television and modern advertising on the young is perhaps best illustrated by the way the head recalled being startled at the matter of fact way some pupils were able to describe some of the unsavoury characters who had on occasion exposed themselves to pupils!

The same year that Mr. McAleese had to contend with public concerns over drugs, the Office for Standards in Education (OFSTED) issued a report of their October inspection. Although the school was praised as "excellent", some of the classroom accommodation was criticised, a comment welcomed by the head, in that it strengthened the case for new buildings. The inspectors were particularly concerned about the continuing use of seven twenty-year old "temporary" classrooms. Among the things praised by the inspectors were the teachers' dedication, the pupils' results, and the community's loyalty.

The concept of the "adventure holiday" that had grown throughout Mrs. Dance's headship, continued to thrive during Mr. McAleese's term of office, and featured regularly in issues of "The Link". The holidays were arranged through a company bearing the name of P.G.L., the founder's initials, and continued to provide memorable adventure holidays for many pupils. Equally memorable were the "themed" holidays and tours, such as the great 1997 music tour of Australia, where the school's musicians gave a series of performances that produced rapturous reviews and immense goodwill. The scale of achievement of the 1997 tour must never be underestimated or forgotten. The school's director of music, Brian Hunt, was also working with the Chamber Orchestra, conducted by Janet Saunders, the Wind Orchestra, conducted by Brian Hunt himself and Mark Robinson, and the Swing Band, conducted by Andy Kemp. These musical activities demonstrated how far the school had come since the days when music had been marginalized.

The school's twenty-three strong swing band made such good progress at this time that they were included in an elite group of ten, chosen from hundreds of prize-winners in a national newspaper's competition. The band's Leeds based peripatetic conductor, Andy Kemp, explained that *"we do blues, swing, Latin American and funk tunes. I try to get them to appreciate all kinds of styles."* As well as contests, the band played at Dublin and Prague. The Swing band, later renamed the Jazz band, is still going strong at the time of writing.

In January 1995, History Teacher Barbara Hibbert found herself in a situation similar to that faced by headmaster Tommy Lusher back in the 1940's, when she organised an exhibition on the Second World War. As has previously been related, Mr. Lusher was startled at one assembly to be faced by rows of boys swathed in machine gun ammunition some brandishing machine gun parts and other warlike implements, which they had salvaged from a downed allied bomber. In Ms. Hibbert's case however, pupil Nick Kendrew satisfied his teacher's request for wartime relics by bringing two bombs which had been retrieved from excavations at New Park and Thirsk.

In the same month that Harrogate Grammar School might have been blown to bits, two students received official recognition of their outstanding rugby talent. Scrum half Martyn Wood was selected to join the team in Lancashire about to face Australia, after he had impressed viewers in trials in Blackpool. Promising prop Neil Liddle was also invited to attend training with the Anglo-Scottish under nineteens' side, after impressing viewers with his talent. Both students were in the sixth form. This was further evidence of Harrogate Grammar School's continuing rugby prowess, a prowess that has too frequently been overshadowed by the publicity accorded to other, and more populist sports.

One of Harrogate's less admirable character traits surfaced in 1995 with local opposition to plans to build a £700,000 astroturf pitch on the Grammar School's playing fields. A joint proposal by Harrogate Grammar School and the Harrogate Hockey and Squash club to build a new facility on the school playing fields was relocated to Granby High School after being blocked by planners, following protests from residents.

Government inability to let teachers get on with the task of teaching surfaced once more in June 1996, when the press announced plans of the education secretary Mrs. Shephard, to make every school in the country consider selection. Accompanied by the usual jargon and self-justification, the politician's comments met little positive reaction in Harrogate, prompting Kevin McAleese to say "*Harrogate Grammar School is likely to remain comprehensive, as it has been since 1973, because of the demands of parents*". One of the reasons for Mr. McAleese's measured response to the thought of more change may have been because he was aware that the Grammar School's high-fliers were already doing extremely well. In January 1996, the Yorkshire Evening Press reported that Harrogate Grammar School had a record number of Oxbridge offers, with three from Oxford and ten from Cambridge, the latter figure said to have been the highest for any state school in Britain. The same month saw the retirement after twenty-two years' service, of Mrs. Kathleen Baker, a popular dinner lady at Arthur's Avenue. Mrs. Baker commented to the Harrogate Advertiser's reporter that pupils no longer tucked into traditional British fare like steak and kidney pudding, but dishes like lasagne, pizza, and colourful vegetarian food!

The 1996 Grammar School Speech day was used by chairman of the Governors Ian

Grant to draw attention to the problem of the deterioration of the school buildings; this was somewhat ironic, in view of the pending discovery of the condition of the Royal Hall, where speech days were held. The problems identified by Mr Grant were (1) temporary laboratories and classrooms were leaking, and expensive to heat and maintain; (2) laboratories needed upgrading; (3) toilets classed as "disgraceful" twenty years ago still needed improving; (4) the insufficiency of hard play areas and inadequacy of all-weather sports areas. Head teacher Kevin McAleese said that the school had now submitted a partnership plan to North Yorkshire Education Department for new science facilities and the removal of temporary classrooms on a joint funding basis. Mr. McAleese also pointed out that during the summer, 91% of students had passed their "A" levels, which was the school's best result yet. He added, *"it really is a pity though that every August young people have their A-level and GCSE successes immediately questioned by politicians who say the results must represent a fall in standards rather than something to celebrate"* When Mr. McAleese made this comment, he was probably unaware that for his remaining years at Harrogate Grammar School, media coverage of educational matters would be increasingly strident, sometimes acrimonious, and often inaccurate. The Yorkshire Post's article on 2nd October 1996 showed one of the Grammar School's "temporary" classrooms, the roof held up with metal struts, and a bucket on a pupil's desk to catch dripping water. The headline read *"Crisis in classroom as school crumbles"*, the whole piece being sensationalist in tone. The following year, an investment of £300,000 was announced, following the Department of Education's approval of borrowing by the North Yorkshire Education authority. A further problem was uncovered in November 2002, when asbestos was discovered in the school, requiring removal by specialist contractors.

The difficulty with criticism of the media in their coverage of Grammar School matters is that a case may be made to show that improvements only arrived after the appearance of dramatic publicity. If this was true, it is also true that the law of diminishing returns must have applied, so that the more frequently dramatic publicity occurred, the less effective it became.

On 7th July 1997, the Yorkshire Post reported that the £300,000 investment would enable the school to convert two classrooms to laboratories, and to purchase the latest equipment. A further four new classrooms could also be built next to the existing technology block, and the hideous temporary classrooms on Otley Road, which had been second hand when purchased in 1976, were at last to be demolished. This was a very important development for the school. December saw the launching of yet another buildings appeal, this time to refurbish the school's lavatories.

Harrogate Grammar School's 1997 triumph at the £300,000 development was tempered by a tragedy. In March, four sixth form students were killed when the car they were all travelling in struck a tree near Beckwithshaw, as they returned to school. Jocelyn Bancroft, Samantha Brearley, Emma Freear and Claire Jennings were commemorated at the school in a variety of ways, including a sundial and the planting of crocuses and rose bushes in a garden of remembrance, a donation to the Stillbirth and Neonatal Death Society, the creation of an annual memorial prize, and the purchase of books and equipment to aid sixth form studies. The generosity of the contributions was eloquent testimony to the community's distress at the tragedy.

In 1998, headteacher Kevin McAleese received the Honour of the CBE for his services to education, barely a few months before the chairman of North Yorkshire's Education Committee, John Dennis, opened the improvements at Harrogate Grammar School, the costs of which had now risen to £369,000. The scheme had evolved to include four new classrooms for the history and religious studies departments, as well as the conversion of existing rooms into state-of-the-art science laboratories. These physical improvements were followed in 1999 by an OFSTED report that singled out the high academic standards achieved by pupils, and awarded the school the grading of "*well above average*". The school's previous OFSTED report of 1994 had led to Harrogate Grammar School being identified as one of the 34 most "outstanding" schools in Britain. Now, in 1999, and after the "*demanding inspection carried out between April 19th-23rd*," inspectors told the school it had made good progress. The report also commended the school's provision for social, moral, and cultural development, relationships among pupils, and between pupils and staff. This official endorsement came at a time when the school's profile was being raised by a variety of yet further publicity, not all of it good.

By 1999, the school's football team was dominating the under-16's football circuit - far gone were the days when enthusiastic footballers were told by their masters that football was only a working class game. Rugby was also flourishing, and fourteen year old Peter Corner was included in the Yorkshire under 15's after what the press described as "*a number of barnstorming displays for his school and his club side, Harrogate*".

Good as 1999 had undoubtedly been for the school, the year also produced a difficulty over the matter of a 1997 legal action from a parent that her son had been the victim of bullying, and that in her opinion, the school had failed to recognize or deal with the issue effectively. The mother, who had taken the North Yorkshire County Council to court over the alleged bullying, was given a £6,000 out of court settlement [without any admission of liability]. A statement issued by Harrogate Grammar School claimed the agreement had been reached to "*save further expense and disruption*". In itself, the allegation of an ineffective response to bullying, was unfortunate, but as nothing compared to what happened next.

On 5th November 1999, the Harrogate Advertiser reported that headteacher Kevin McAleese had been obliged to call in the police when he was subjected to a string of hate mail, which, as might be expected from such cowardly communications, was anonymous. Copies of the letters were sent to people associated with local education, prominent figures, and the local newspaper. One letter claimed that the recent £6,000 payment to the mother who had made the complaint about bullying, had left the County Council with a £22,000 bill which would have to be passed on to the school. This last accusation came at a time when Local Education Authority cuts of £100,000 had produced a fall in income for the school, and when a request was being considered to ask parents to make a voluntary contribution of £5 per term. The press noted that the parent involved in the bullying allegations had condemned the anonymous letters, and wanted to be disassociated from them totally. Later, the press reported that Mr. McAleese had been the subject of a further spate of hate mail.

Despite the upset from this correspondence, Kevin McAleese pressed on with, and was successful with his plan to take advantage of the government's initiative to allow selected schools to obtain specialist college status, and with it, extra funding. The King James' Grammar School at Knaresborough, and Harrogate's St. John Fisher School, had already applied for, and obtained special status (the former as the area's specialist technology centre, and the latter as the area's arts college). When Harrogate Grammar School's case was submitted, after being coordinated by deputy head, Dr.Alun Rees, it was for the school to become a language college – the first of its kind in North Yorkshire. In 1999, the school had already been awarded international school status, thanks to the efforts of teacher Christine Howson, and had ties with schools in Europe, America and North Africa.

The submission was to enable Harrogate Grammar School to participate in the government's plan to expand the number of specialised schools across the country with specific curriculum activities, including technology, sports, the arts, and languages. In an interview with the Harrogate Advertiser, Dr Rees commented that *"the Government initiative (is) designed to benefit all the town's young people and aims to provide the excellent communication skills required by business and industry and for young people's success beyond school. Our aim is to improve quality and a wide breadth of languages for industry and the job market, which is increasingly favouring languages. We hope to go beyond the traditional range to include Japanese, Chinese, and Russian...and to broaden students' individual horizons."* Language College status would not only benefit Harrogate Grammar School, but other schools in the district, in that primary schools would be able to have lunch-time or after school classes, and there would be support for teachers, and after-hours classes for the local community.

The edition of the Harrogate Advertiser for 29th June 2001 carried an announcement that Harrogate Grammar School had been awarded an extra £500,000 in Government funding, after achieving the much-coveted status of specialist school: this was a considerable achievement. The school was to be recognised as a language college from September 2001. The Advertiser's good news appeared only four months after Mr. McAleese had to contend with the bad news that the County Council was again set to cut core school budgets by 1.2% at the very time when state secondary schools were faced with the costs of introducing the new post-16 curriculum. Commenting in the Harrogate Advertiser, Mr. McAleese said he faced losing his school's entire financial reserves in two years. The school had received £70,000 extra in standards grants directly from the government, but stood to lose about £50,000 through Council cuts. Head teachers throughout the county were warned that they faced the worst ever financial position [although whoever wrote this clearly had not lived through the great depression of the 1930's].

The school "house" system, abandoned in the 1960's, when the growing influence of those with a craven fear of rank and hierarchy pretended to see the dreaded public school image in such competing organisms, was revived, thanks to the deputy head and Oxford graduate Alan Boddy and his supporters. The old house colour system was re-introduced: red, blue, yellow and green, a name choice intended to be temporary, but made permanent by lack of anything better. The revived house system proved to be a great success, re-introducing a healthy competition for youngsters about to enter a world in which competition was an inescapable fact of life. Each form joined one house, and pupils could then contribute their own points to the communal pot, a valuable lesson in striving for social, as well as individual, success. House rivalry in such things as music, drama and sport became highly popular, enhancing the communal life of the school, while developing that of the individual pupil. Alan Boddy, who had been with the school since 1971, retired in 2002.

"*I feel I'm leaving at the right time*" was the newspaper headline that accompanied an article in the Harrogate Advertiser of 22nd June 2001, announcing Kevin McAleese's decision to take early retirement. News of the head's decision seems to have come as a surprise to the Advertiser, who commented that it might be seen as "premature." In retrospect however, it should have been obvious that a man with Mr McAleese's abilities might feel that after ten years at the helm, and the crowning success of the language college award, the time had indeed come to say farewell. Along with the gaining of special status as a language college in June 2001, Kevin McAleese felt that highlights of his headship were the 1992 opening of the Newton Wing (begun in 1989 during Mrs. Dance's headship) which had been funded with 50% contribution from parents' fund raising activities and matching the 50% received from the Local Educational Authority, and the 1998 opening of the new Humanities Block.

Two of the last photographs of Kevin McAleese to appear in the Harrogate press were on 13th July and 7th September 2001; the former photograph showed an immaculately dressed Mr. McAleese, surrounded by pupils who had taken part successfully in the National Mathematics challenge. The September picture showed the head teacher being presented with the "Investors in People" award by M.P. Phil Willis, on behalf of the North Yorkshire Business and Education Partnership.

Shortly before Mr. McAleese arrived at the Grammar School, the Governors had taken the decision to abolish the traditional brown uniform for girls. A similar decision was pending to abolish the black blazers for boys. As Mr. McAleese believed in the wearing of blazers, he persuaded the Governors to change their minds about abolishing such apparel. From September 1992, years seven, eight and nine had to wear blazers, but years ten and eleven were allowed to replace the blazer with a black pullover. The sixth form had been allowed to wear what they liked for some time, including jeans and t-shirts, which produced the anomalous situation that a casually dressed sixth form prefect could reprimand a junior child for not wearing a blazer! Kevin McAleese changed this, got rid of jeans, and made the wearing of ties compulsory. A working party had recommended the abolition of jeans in school and despite some staff opposition, the move was accepted. Mr. McAleese recalled that one enterprising boy had told his mother that ties were now compulsory, and that he was required to own five different Versace ties, one for each day of the week!

Some people have voiced the opinion that standards of school uniform declined at the Grammar School during the late 20th century [a phenomenon that appears to have been national]. As the photographs of Mr. McAleese reveal, he himself always had the highest sartorial standards, so one possible explanation for the alleged decline of pupils' appearance may be that the administrative nature of the head's job prevented him from regularly seeing the appearance of any alleged offenders.

Kevin McAleese's successor, Dr. Limbert, has recalled that he first visited Harrogate Grammar School on a Saturday, when the buildings and grounds looked at their best; it was this favourable impression that determined Philip Limbert to apply for the headship. From the start, Dr. Limbert knew that the maintenance of school discipline was essential if the staff were to be confident of their ability to control a class, and he determined to encourage staff to exercise such control. His fresh look at school uniform and behaviour was very much following initiatives by Mary Dance and Kevin McAleese, and if the outcome may have been different, the motivation was the same. Dr. Limbert has never made any secret of his intention of developing Harrogate Grammar School into a model of post-comprehensive education. The Harrogate Advertiser for 19th April 2002 published an interview with the Grammar School's new head teacher, who did not pull his punches, and gave simple, direct answers to reporter

Anastasia Weiner. *"My question to the pupils was what to do with an absolutely excellent school ?"*, Dr. Limbert's answer being *"turn it into the best school in Britain..."* Nor were these mere words, as Dr. Limbert began his reign at Harrogate Grammar School with energetic action against all that to his eyes appeared sloppy or undesirable in the behaviour and appearance of pupils. By the summer of 2003, Dr.Limbert had calculated that he was 85% towards his intention of exercising 100% disciplinary control.

Philip Limbert came to Harrogate fresh from a high-achieving school in Wakefield, after beginning his teaching career in West Yorkshire at the West Leeds High School, Armley. Posts then followed at Maidstone, Chelmsford, Holland Park School in London [where he was deputy head], and the specialist technology school at Ossett, Wakefield. During his first year at Harrogate Grammar School, 18% of all the school's sixteen year olds obtained grades "A" or "A*" in their GCSE's : a good result, but one that Dr. Limbert knew could be improved. The ambitious Dr. Limbert has spoken unambiguously of his desire to make Harrogate Grammar School the best comprehensive school in Britain. The attainment of this desire is feasible in that the school has a critical mass of high-attaining pupils who are being educated in an institution that has always been capable of innovation. Parental cooperation is obviously essential, and the head teacher wants the school to be well regarded by parents, who must feel that the education their child will receive at the Grammar School will be at least as good as any paid for at a private school. The philosophy driving this education is to ensure that each child is given the best life-chance possible.

November 2002 saw the completion of Harrogate Grammar School's transformation into a leading language college. The three month renovations included not only 32 new computer terminals, attractive new lighting and colour schemes [along with certain structural alterations, providing larger, smarter classrooms] but two television monitors, showing foreign language broadcasts, set up in the school's reception area. Harrogate Grammar School was set to take up the challenges of the twenty-first century.

In the pre-Thatcher years it was said that teachers enjoyed maximum support and minimum accountability, whereas under Margaret Thatcher, teachers enjoyed minimum support and maximum accountability. Dr. Limbert's challenge will be to fulfil his vision for the school within the wider national concern to balance these states with both support for far less able pupils and accountability.

Postscript

With the completion of the author's task of relating Harrogate Grammar School's history over the century between 1903 and 2003, there remain only two tasks outstanding: a summary and a warning.

The summary is soon written. Harrogate Grammar School's centenary is an appropriate occasion to reflect on the institution's successes. Those successes have been achieved by a single minded pursuit of excellence, an excellence achieved with breathtaking regularity thanks to the combined work of pupils, teachers, parents, governors and heads. The school's success has all too often been despite, rather than because of, the involvement of outside authorities such as national government. Teachers left to teach will only enhance the Grammar School's record of excellence; teachers forced by society to become social workers or administrators will only reduce it.

The warning is of a threat that has already arrived. A new malaise has crept over mankind, the key manifestation being of timidity. Everywhere, humanity cowers beneath the bed sheets, bound by the silken ropes of political correctness, afraid of threatening deeds, words or even thoughts. The result is usually a deadly inaction that hinders new adventure and closes unexplored frontiers. The paralysing justification for this withering of man is that it makes the spiritually timid feel safe.

Harrogate Grammar School's future success will come from its ability to develop the full potential of each pupil, and not just those of its charges who may meet the tenets of either the politically correct moment, or an elite minority obsessed with high academic qualifications. After having experienced the changes of its first century, the school has never been so well prepared to guide its pupils forward to take up the challenges of the twenty-first century. It is the author's impartial opinion that Harrogate Grammar School, located in the finest town in England, is now poised to become the nation's finest state school, with an even brighter future.

Selective subject index
excluding names of pupils and teachers, other than heads

Acts of parliament – 1870 7, 127,
Acts of parliament – 1880 7,
Acts of parliament – 1891 8,
Acts of parliament – 1902 9,
Acts of Parliament – 1918 24,
Acts of Parliament – 1936 31,
Acts of Parliament – 1944 51, 104, 140,
Acts of Parliament – 1980 136,
Acts of Parliament – 1986 140,
Acts of Parliament – 1988 140, 147,
Adventure holidays 136, 150,
Air raid precautions 47, 48,
Alchohol 149,
Art 38, 39, 42, 110, 121, 132,
Arthur's Avenue 33, 34, 47,
Astroturf pitch 151
Blyth Nook 25, 27,
Board of Education 18, 28,
Book binding 108,
Boxing 15,
Bullying 153,
Bursar 143,
Cadet corps 42, 43, 50, 51, 123,
Cadets' firing range 104,
Car accidents 152, 153,
Caretaker 48, 109,
Charitable work 104, 135, 141, 147,
Chemistry 21, 28, 39, 106, 123,
Class sizes 26, 31,
Cleaning 143,
Comics 108,
Commercial studies 37,
Comprehensive education 125, 126, 129, 130, 131, 133, 144, 151, 156,
Computers 141, 142, 143, 145,
Cookery 30,
Cricket 19, 29, 31, 49,
Cricket pavilion 48,
Crowther report 119,
Cumberland House 26,
Curriculum 14, 16, 28, 41, 51, 107-8, 110, 140, 154,
Debating society 118, 149,
Dental care 30, 31,
Dickens, Charles – works of 112,
Dictation 41
Discipline 17, 18, 102, 135, 157,
Domestic Science 28, 29, 104, 110,
Drama 28, 30,

Dramatic productions 21, 28, 113, 132, 139,
Dramatic Society 19,
Drugs 141, 149,
Education committee 11, 26, 27,
English 28, 30, 39, 52, 101, 108, 122, 132, 134, 139,
Evacuees 45, 52,
Examinations 11, 16, 18, 23, 52, 105, 108,110, 112, 125, 130, 131, 137, 139,
Exquisite Burden 15, 16, 17, 19, 128,
Extra-curricular activities 19, 38, 104, 113, 131, 141,
Fences & railings 27, 47,
Football 19, 29, 31, 51, 102, 114, 121, 153,
French 28, 39, 106, 110, 122,
Gender divisions 13, 28, 37, 41, 48, 134,
Geography 15, 28, 29, 38, 39, 41, 107, 110,
George vi coronation procession 43,
German 38, 108, 110, 126, 128, 145,
Girl Guides 22,
Girls' Air training corps 47,
Goodrick's fields 16, 25, 29,
Governors 15, 19, 23, 25, 26, 33, 37, 119, 136, 146, 148, 151,
Grammar School – architecture 32,
Grammar School – catchment area 130,
Grammar School – extensions 129, 130, 133, 143, 145, 150, 152, 157.
Grammar School – name 32, 111, 131,
Grammar School – opening 32,
Grammar School – repairs 147, 148, 152,
Grammar School – security 150,
Grove Road School 8,
Gymnasium 16, 48, 52, 108,
Hand-press 41,
Headmaster Carr, H.C.C. 35-44, 46, 52, 101, 106, 109, 112-120, 147,
Headmaster Hill, E.G. 121-137,
Headmaster Lusher, T. 26, 35, 45-52, 52, 109, 113,
Headmaster Thoseby, A.E. 14, 17, 24, 28, 32, 147,
Headmaster Watson, T. 9, 13, 14, 26, 43, 44,
Head Teacher Dance, M. 138-144, 156,
Head Teacher Limbert, P. 156-157,
Head Teacher McAleese, K 145-156,
History 28, 40, 50, 102, 107, 110, 122, 127, 131, 150,
Hockey 19, 31,

Honours board 15,
House systems 104, 155,
Humanities block 155,
Induction ritual 45,
Inspections 14, 18, 40, 42, 109, 110,
Inspectors' reports 14, 40, 109, 110,
Kitchens 29, 104,
Land labour 103, 115,
Language college 154, 155, 157,
Languages 126, 128, 138,
Latin 28, 39, 41, 102, 108, 110, 115,
Library 109, 112, 123, 130, 147,
Link (The) 144, 150,
Local Education Authorities 10, 26, 51, 140, 143, 147, 148, 154, 155,
Local Education Authorities – "opting out" controversy 148
Magic Society 104,
Mathematics 26, 28, 29, 35, 39, 41, 108, 110, 113, 114, 124, 131, 134,
Mechanics 36,
Mechanics' Institutes 8,
Medical care 30
Memorial plaque 108,
Metalwork 46, 101, 108,
Morris dancing 15,
Mountaineering 38, 107, 115, 117,
Municipal Secondary School 10, 11, 13, 14, 16, 23, 25, 28, 31,
Music 28, 104, 108, 110, 112, 116, 118, 119, 134, 150,
Needlework 36, 108,
Net-ball 21,
Newton wing 145, 155,
Otley Road 16, 25,
Parents' association 127, 129, 130, 147,
Pastoral care 139,
Photographic society 104,
Physical education 26, 28, 40, 50, 102, 108,
Physics 28, 39, 123, 124, 134, 139, 142,
Play grounds 14,
Playing fields 15, 29, 116,
Pottery making 109,
Prefectorate 45,
Prizes 49, 113, 117, 136,
Punishments – corporal 17, 102, 126, 135, 140,
Punishments – detention 17, 21,
Pupil numbers 11, 12, 32, 35, 37, 38, 40, 42, 44, 52, 109, 119, 120, 123, 125, 133, 142,
Pupil-teachers 13,

Pupils associations & reunions 15, 19, 32,
Queen Victoria's Diamond Jubilee 9,
Refugees 20, 21, 45,
Religious instruction 10, 28, 40, 110, 139,
Reports, government 27, 28, 43, 126, 153,
Rugby 101, 115, 121, 127, 131, 151, 153,
Scholarships 24, 105, 112, 114, 121,
School bell 116,
School Board 7, 10,
School certificate examination 23, 109,
School clock 48, 147,
School constitution 52,
School furniture 118,
School league tables 144, 146,
School leaving age 24, 27, 31, 109,
School magazine 14, 21, 52, 105, 112, 121, 129,
School meals 13, 15, 103, 142, 151,
School milk 29, 103,
School motto 42,
School uniforms 29, 32, 103, 110, 116, 122, 141, 146, 156,
Science 108, 110, 130, 131, 134,
Scouts 117,
Sixth form 125, 130, 136, 137, 148,
Smoking 28, 122, 133, 149,
Spanish 108, 110,
Special needs pupils 131, 138,
Speech day 138,
Sports 16, 19, 38, 101, 117, 131,
Sports board 17,
Staff gowns 123,
Staff numbers 13, 101, 109, 123,
Staff rooms 28, 133,
Streaming 125, 129, 131, 132, 133, 134,
Street Talk 142
Swimming instruction 15, 31, 104, 113, 138, 147,
Talking Newspaper 136, 137,
Technical College 8, 9, 10, 11,
University entrants 107, 121, 125, 130, 131, 133, 134, 136, 137, 146, 151,
Victoria Cross winners 15, 19, 22, 46,
War deaths 22,
Wetherby film 139,
Winter of 1947 – the great freeze 105, 106,
Wood-work 18, 36, 40, 101, 117, 118,
Woods linens 15,
World War One 20 –24
World War Two 45-52, 108, 150,